SLOYD

BY

GUSTAF LARSSON
PRINCIPAL SLOYD TRAINING SCHOOL
BOSTON, MASSACHUSETTS

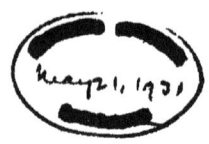

TT187
.L315

HARVARD UNIVERSITY
GRADUATE SCHOOL OF EDUCATION
MONROE C. GUTMAN LIBRARY

Copyright
By Gustaf Larsson
1902

TO
MRS. QUINCY A. SHAW
IN GRATEFUL RECOGNITION
OF HER INSPIRING
SYMPATHY AND CO-OPERATION
IN MY WORK

PREFACE.

The following papers have been collected and printed at the request of several friends, who have felt that the educational character and the universal need of Sloyd should be better and more generally understood. These papers have been read at different times and places, and consequently contain some unavoidable repetition.

Unfortunately, Sloyd has often been superficially judged from its outward symbols only, while the vital principles for which it stands have been overlooked. It is hoped that this little publication may help to convince teachers and other promoters of education that the principles of Sloyd are broad and universal, and that as an effective educational agent it deserves a place in our schools.

I am greatly indebted to my fellow-workers for valuable aid and suggestions in preparing these papers, especially to the teachers and friends of the Sloyd Training School, who have earnestly co-operated with me in the work.

GUSTAF LARSSON.

SLOYD TRAINING SCHOOL,
BOSTON, MASSACHUSETTS,
　　May, 1902.

CONTENTS.

Paper		Page
I.	EDUCATIONAL MANUAL TRAINING OR SLOYD. Illustrated. Read before the National Summer School, Glens Falls, N.Y., July, 1891	9
II.	SLOYD FOR ELEMENTARY SCHOOLS, AS CONTRASTED WITH THE RUSSIAN SYSTEM OF MANUAL TRAINING. Illustrated. Read at the International Congress of Education of the World's Columbian Exposition, Chicago, July 26, 1893,	19
III.	SLOYD AS A MEANS OF GENERAL EDUCATION. Read at a meeting of the California State Teachers' Association in Stockton, Dec. 26, 1893	27
IV.	A FEW FACTS CONCERNING THE WORK OF THE SLOYD TRAINING SCHOOL, BOSTON. Illustrated. Presented at the Graduating Exercises, May 25, 1895	35
V.	SLOYD. Read before the Connecticut State Teachers' Association at New Haven, Oct. 16, 1896	39
VI.	SOME OBSERVATIONS ON MANUAL TRAINING IN EUROPE AND AMERICA. Read at the meeting of the Committee on Manual Training of the New England Educational Workers, Nov. 11, 1896	47
VII.	MANUAL TRAINING AS A FACTOR IN PHYSICAL EDUCATION. Illustrated. Read before the Boston Society for Advancement of Physical Education, Feb. 11, 1897	58
VIII.	MANUAL TRAINING. Read at the meeting of the State Teachers' Association at Concord, N.H., Oct. 20, 1900,	63
IX.	AN ANSWER TO SOME OF THE COMMON OBJECTIONS TO SLOYD. Read at the meeting of the Marlborough Teachers' Association, Feb. 10, 1902. Chart and Illustrations	69

I.

EDUCATIONAL MANUAL TRAINING, OR SLOYD.

Paper read at the meeting of the Teachers' National Summer School at Glens Falls, N.Y., July, 1891.

In beginning to speak upon manual training, and especially that form of manual training known as Sloyd, I must ask your indulgence, as I still have difficulty in using your language. If, however, you will give me your kind attention and patient sympathy, I will try to tell you something of what I have learned on this subject.

Most of the exponents of the various systems of manual training agree that education is the end to be obtained, but they differ as to the meaning of the word "education." Some think that it refers only to a training for purely mental development, while others think it refers to a training for the sake of getting a livelihood. Most progressive thinkers and writers upon the subject, however, claim that the hand should be employed, as a tool of the brain, to supplement prevailing methods and to develop general power.

This is often called the "new education"; but the history of education, as far back as the fifteenth century, and even long before, gives us ideas similar to those expressed by our modern leaders. In order to show that the aim of educational manual training is but an outgrowth of the aim of general education, as it has for a long time been understood, I shall quote from several recognized authorities: —

Johann Amos Comenius (1592-1671), who has been called the "father of modern education," says in some of his numerous treatises on the educational value of manual work: "Let everything be communicated through the senses, and turned to present use. Let nothing be prescribed as a memory-task that has not previously been thoroughly understood. Leave nothing, until it has been impressed by means of the ear, the eye, the tongue, the hand. Let nothing be learned by authority, but by demonstration, sensible and rational. Above all, never teach words without things, even in the vernacular; and whatever the pupils see, hear, taste, or touch, let them name. The tongue and the intelligence should advance on parallel lines. For the beginning of knowledge is from pure sense, not from words; and truth and certitude are testified to by the evidence of the senses. The senses are the most faithful stewards of the memory. The study of language should run parallel with the study of things, especially in youth, for we desire to *form men, not parrots.*"

By this we see that Comenius, who lived in the seventeenth century, had a clear idea of that for which our educational reformers to-day are striving.

Jean Jacques Rousseau (1712–1778), who also preached the "gospel of natural education," says: "Instead of fastening the child to his books, if I employ him in a workshop, his hands work to the advantage of his brain, he becomes a philosopher and thinks himself only a workman. Indeed, this exercise has other advantages of which I will speak hereafter; and we shall see how from the workings of philosophy one can elevate himself to the true function of manhood." "Work!" he says, "if not from necessity, then because of the dignity of work. One must work like a peasant and think like a philosopher, unless he be as worthless as a savage. The great secret of education is to make the exercises of the body and of the spirit serve each to relieve the other."

Frederick Fröbel (1782–1852), founder of the kindergarten, has of course made familiar the idea that manual work should be used continually as an effective means of education, on which principle, indeed, his system entirely depends. To quote Fröbel, in this connection, would be to quote everything he has written; for we should find, as his leading thought, this text: "Man only understands thoroughly that which he is able to produce."

The eminent English scholar and scientist, Sir James Chrichton Browne, tells us that certain portions of the brain are developed between the ages of four and fourteen years by manual exercises alone. He also says, "It is plain that the highest functional activity of these motor centres is a thing to be aimed at with a view to general mental power as well as with a view to muscular expertness; and as the hand centres hold a prominent place among the motor centres, and are in relation with an organ which in prehension, in touch, and in a thousand different combinations of movement, adds enormously to our intellectual resources, thoughts, and sentiments, it is plain that the highest possible functional activity of these hand centres is of paramount importance not less to mental grasp than to industrial success." Again he says, "Depend upon it that much of the confusion of thought, awkwardness, bashfulness, stutterings, stupidity, and irresolution which we encounter in the world, and even in highly educated men and women, is dependent on defective or misdirected muscular training, and that the thoughtful and diligent cultivation of this is conducive to breadth of mind as well as to breadth of shoulders."

In a treatise on "The Influence of Manual Training on Character," Dr. Adler makes a strong point when he calls attention to some of the dangers to boys arising from weakness of will, such as sensuality, vacillation of purpose, "mental incoherency, indolence, a deficiency in the sense of shame"; and he then shows how the will may be strengthened by that training which gives the power of adapting means to ends,— of giving a "connectedness between ideas,"—and this, he says, can most readily be done by "manual training," because manual training is interesting to the young,—even to the young criminal.

"By manual training," says Dr. Adler, "we cultivate the intellect in close and inseparable connection with action. Manual training consists of a series of actions, which are controlled by the mind and which always react on it." He then points out how the attention and interest is excited in the child's mind in making something of real use. He shows how the variety of manipulation, in making an object, constantly stimulates interest, and how at the same time the carefully graded exercises teach the pupil in an elementary way "the lesson of subordinating minor ends to a major end"; and when, at last, with triumph, the child contemplates his finished work, the pleasure of achievement comes in to crown his experience, and this sense of achievement leaves in his mind a sense of pleasant enthusiasm which will stimulate him to similar work in the future. "The child," he says, "that has once acquired, in connection with the making of a box, the habits just described, has mastered the secret of a strong will, and will be able to apply the same habits in other directions and on other occasions."

Dr. Adler further says: "I have thus far attempted to show how the will can be made strong. But a strong will is not necessarily a good will. It is true there are influences in manual training, as it has been described, which are favorable to a virtuous disposition. Squareness in things is not without relation to squareness in action and thinking. A child that has learned to be exact — that is, truthful in his work — will be inclined to be scrupulous and truthful in his speech, in his thoughts, and in his acts."

I like to dwell upon the moral influence of the work which is so effectively emphasized by Dr. Adler, because I believe that without definite and adequate provision for the moral growth of children in elementary schools the higher educational institutions can hardly reach the desired standard. The moral effect of manual training is often apparent in the child's behavior and in his respect for his skilful schoolmates. Some teachers have observed that more accurate thinking and improved methods of study, especially in arithmetic, have resulted from manual training. It gives a child independent standards. He loves good work, likes to be useful, prefers occupation to idleness; and thus the germs of good citizenship are planted at the time most favorable to growth and development. A healthy impetus is also given to the moral nature by the improved physical condition resulting from this training. A freer circulation promotes health, increases happiness, and opens a way to the best impulses of the heart. The youthful energy, which is often too much confined to the exercise of the brain alone, finds, by the use of tools, a natural outlet in the bodily powers.

I could, if it seemed best, fill my paper with telling quotations and illustrations; and, if I seem already to borrow too much from others who have spoken on this subject, it is because they have expressed the ideas which I hold better than my limited knowledge of the English language enables me to do. You will see the same leading thought in the writings of such men as Locke, Franke, Basedow, Salzmann, Pestalozzi, Herbart, and other great promoters of education. Most of the educational reformers to-day seem to be working in the same spirit. It is indeed interesting to me to find with what intelligence and thoroughness the subject has been discussed by many of the leading men in this country; and it is all the more surprising to find how little in harmony with the theories of these reformers are the prevailing methods of manual training.

It will be seen that manual training should mean much more than training of hand and eye. It should mean the intelligent exercise of the whole body. The restlessness of the children should be turned to good account. The sedentary occupations, such as knitting, sewing, paper work, clay modelling, etc., are good as far as they go; but there is an unanswered cry in every child's nature which will not be satisfied until every muscle is brought into vigorous action.

It becomes apparent, then, that the *methods* of manual training must be carefully considered with a view to the accomplishment of all these ends even from a physical point of view; and it is a striking peculiarity of Sloyd that the gymnastic value of the work is carefully considered in the choice and use of tools and material as well as in the progression and alternation of exercises.

My own experience as a teacher in this work has been chiefly with children of eleven to fifteen years of age, and I believe that this is the right age at which to get the greatest benefit from manual training with wood-working tools. Children of this age, while they are likely to have sufficient strength for the vigorous muscular work required, are also more susceptible to moral influences than older children. It has been urged that Sloyd should be employed with even younger children on account of their impressibility; and, to meet this demand, I have planned a suggestive course of work, consisting of simple exercises and a moderate number of tools. There is no reason, when time and opportunity permit, why Sloyd methods should not be adapted to the need of both younger and older pupils.

I have many times been asked what the word Sloyd means, and why it is used in preference to your English words "manual training" and "wood-work," or "carpentry." The word Slöjd comes from an old Swedish adjective "Slög," meaning skilful, handy, or deft, and from it comes the noun Slöjd, or English Sloyd. The name Sloyder (Swedish Slöjdare) is applied to a person possessing a certain dexterity of hand, without being in any sense an artisan.

Sloyd has had an interesting evolution in Sweden.

When the Sloyd question was first considered in that country, it was not so much considered for its educational value as it was an experiment in national economy. As Sweden was not a rich country, but one which depended mostly on agriculture, it was of great importance that the farmers and their help should be able to manufacture for themselves all kinds of domestic articles, and this they had done for many years; but in 1872 it was found that there were only five provinces out of the twenty-four where this old home industry was kept alive. The chief cause for this decadence was the introduction of machinery to take the place of handicraft. Things which the farmers used to make in their homes, during the long dark winters, could now be bought very cheaply. The decadence of the old home industry showed its effect, not only from the economic standpoint, but also in a decline in the *moral and physical health of the communities*. This was recognized as so serious a danger that the provincial societies made strong effort to re-establish the " hem Slöjd " (or home Sloyd); and a grant of 2,500 crowns was made by the government in 1872, which was afterward raised to 10,000 and again to 20,000 for this purpose.

In 1875 the Royal Academy appointed two civil engineers to organize temporary courses in Sloyd, for the benefit of teachers and others interested, in different parts of Sweden. The government also raised a sum of 15,000 crowns intended solely to aid those public schools in which Sloyd was taught. Unfortunately, the first efforts were not very successful. Several kinds of handiwork were taught, such as fret-sawing, basket-making, cooper's and wheelwright's work, etc., but the work received more attention than the worker. The spirit of the teaching was too technical. In the year 1872, however, a more rational course of Sloyd was worked out by one for whom I entertain the highest regard.

It is to Herr Otto Salomon, Nääs, Sweden, that the educational Sloyd movement in Sweden and other countries owes its greatest advancement and greatest value. Perhaps I can do no better than to give you Herr Salomon's presentation of the aims and methods of Sloyd: —

" Instilling a taste for and love of work in general.

" Inspiring a respect for rough, honest, bodily labor.

" Training in habits of order, exactness, cleanliness, and neatness.

" Accustoming to attention, industry, and perseverance.

" Promoting the development of the physical powers.

" Affording a training of the eye in the sense of form.

" Manual training must exercise the thinking power, and not be purely mechanical.

" There must be no division of labor, and so it must correspond with the capabilities of the child.

" As one of the aims is to cultivate general dexterity of hand, the material must be employed which permits of the use of numerous manipulations and of various tools."

In the choice of methods and arrangement of models the following points should be considered: —

1. The series must progress without break from the easy to the difficult, from the simple to the complex.

2. There must be a refreshing variety both in the exercises, tools and models.

3. At the beginning of the series the models should be capable of being quickly executed, and by degrees models that require a larger time should be given.

4. In making the first models, only a small number of tools is to be used. As the work progresses, the number of tools and manipulations should be gradually increased.

5. The models must follow in such progressive order that by means of the preceding ones the pupils may attain the necessary aptitude to make the succeeding ones without direct help.

6. The models must be so graduated that at every stage the pupil is able to make an exact copy, not merely an approximate one.

7. At first the knife as the fundamental tool should be most used.

You will perhaps be interested to hear a few words in regard to the first efforts to make Sloyd known in Boston.

Having studied Sloyd in Sweden at the well-known school at Nääs, in the double capacity of pupil and teacher, I felt that a knowledge of the system should be more widely diffused than it then was.

During my studies I was more and more impressed by the importance of the work; and being convinced that a broader opportunity would not only enlarge its sphere of usefulness, but also help to develop unrealized possibilities of Sloyd, I concluded to visit America, hoping to interest school boards and other promoters of education, and that their sympathy and interest would result in the establishment here of schools for Sloyd. With this aim in view, I gave up temporarily my position as teacher in one of the Swedish schools, and came to the United States, arriving in Boston on the first day of July, 1888.

Through the mediation of one of my countrymen who had preceded me, I was made known to one who is well known for her public-spirited, philanthropic interest in public education; and after only one week's stay in Boston I was engaged to teach Sloyd to children in two private summer schools. During that time I had the opportunity to plan, make, and test a course of models, twenty-five in number, and suitable, as I thought, for American children above eleven years of age. In the teaching of this first course I also made working drawings on the blackboard for the children to read, and also cards of constructive drawings which should be used to precede and accompany the work. As you will see by illustrations, this course consists of objects which would be considered useful by an American boy. With this end in view, I also tried to keep the gradual progression of exercises and tools which are characteristic of the Swedish work. As I had come to

America for the purpose of interesting teachers and other promoters of education in Sloyd rather than to teach children, I at first sent out invitations to public schoolteachers of Boston to visit an exhibition of Sloyd work, and at that time I secured only the names of those teachers who were interested in the study of the subject. Free lessons were offered to teachers in classes established by Mrs. Quincy A. Shaw, which were to be given after regular school hours, in the evening, and on Saturdays. Thus the work began in a tentative way.

At the beginning of the second year, fifty public schoolteachers were taking the normal course; and in the fall of the same year the number was increased to one hundred and twenty. Meanwhile sixty pupils from one of the Boston grammar schools were placed under my instruction; and now (1891), in the third year of my work in Boston, in the school under my care, one hundred and sixty teachers were studying the modified Swedish methods, besides two hundred public school pupils weekly.

This system of Sloyd is now * being tested (1891) in several Boston schools and institutions, including the Perkins Institution for the Blind and the Horace Mann School for the Deaf. In these, as well as in a large private school, both boys and girls are engaged in the work.

* At the present time, 1902, twenty-seven graduates of the Sloyd Training School are teaching Sloyd to over six thousand boys in the Boston public schools, where it now forms a part of the regular work.

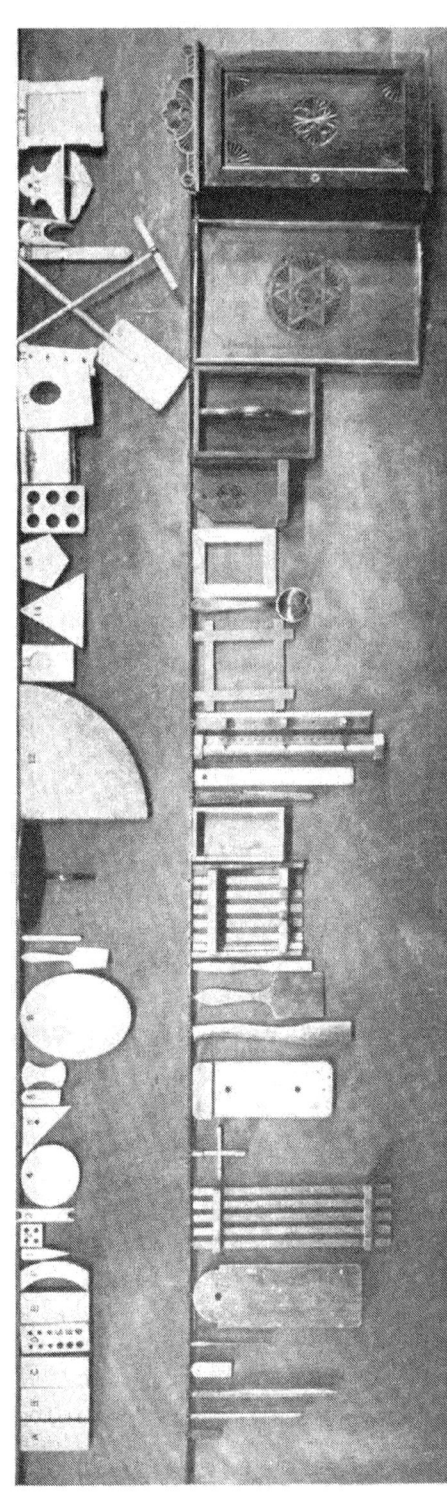

A.—COURSE OF ELEMENTARY SLOYD MODELS USED IN 1889.
B.—COURSE FOR GRAMMAR GRADES, MADE AND USED IN 1888.

THESE MODELS, HAVING ALL BEEN MORE OR LESS CHANGED, SHOW THAT SLOYD DOES NOT STAND FOR A FIXED COURSE OF MODELS OR EXERCISES BUT THAT IT IS A GROWTH. IT NECESSITATES CONSTANT STUDY OF EXISTING NEEDS AND READINESS TO ADAPT TOOLS, MATERIALS, AND OBJECTS TO SUCH NEEDS.

II.

SLOYD FOR ELEMENTARY SCHOOLS, AS CONTRASTED WITH THE RUSSIAN SYSTEM OF MANUAL TRAINING.

Paper read at the International Congress of Education of the World's Columbian Exposition, Chicago, July 26, 1893.

I have been invited to say a few words about Sloyd, and especially to consider in what ways its methods are different from those of the Russian system of manual training.

Although I believe in educational manual training for all ages, I have concentrated my thought chiefly on work for boys and girls in elementary schools (children of eleven to fifteen years). The reason for this is that the kindergarten and primary schools have been well supplied with occupations, and the technical high schools have long been established.

The question is often asked: "Why use the word 'Sloyd'? Would not a name more familiar to American ears, such as manual training or carpentry, answer the purpose just as well?" It might be replied that this system had its origin in Sweden, where it had been practised for over twenty years, and that the word "Sloyd" at once suggests its history, and gives credit where credit is due; also, that the fact of its being an unusual word attracts attention, and stimulates inquiry and study. But the main reason for retaining the name "Sloyd" lies in the fact that the word has no equivalent in the English language. The expression "manual training" is too indefinite, as it may be *manual only*, and given only for industrial purposes, while the term "carpentry" entirely fails to explain the full and true purpose of Sloyd.

The word "Sloyd" means manual training for the sake of general development, physical, mental, and moral, and it also means that kind of hand-work which will best stimulate the right kind of head-work; and, as this word alone sets forth the true aim of this system, it seems desirable that it be retained.

The general aim of Sloyd, then, is the moral, mental, and physical development of the pupil, the mental development being secured by help of the physical. In other words, a definite effort is made to provide such manual work as will arouse a mental enthusiasm, the value of which will be felt in all the intellectual work of the school. I am aware of the fact that this is the aim of all truly educational manual training. The difference is found here in means and methods.

The question now is, What are the best methods? Obviously, that method is best which secures the greatest interest of the pupil, independently of the teacher, and which provides a progressive series of exercises of the greatest educational value physically and mentally. The methods of the Swedish Sloyd system are based upon the following ideas:—

1. The exercises should follow in a progressive order, from the easy to the difficult, from the simple to the complex, without any injurious break, and with such carefully graded demands on the powers of both mind and hand that the development of the two shall be equal and simultaneous. This duality of progression is an essential feature of Sloyd. It cannot be shown in any course of manual work: nothing but careful observation of the child's gain of power in many directions will show the result aimed at.

2. The exercises should admit of the greatest possible variety: they must avoid any tendency either to too great *mental* tension, confusion, or *physical* strain. There is a danger here, not always recognized; for it takes a careful observer and a true teacher to discover that a model may be

at the same time too easy for the hand and too difficult for the mind; while the hand may be well trained by a model which gives the mind little or nothing to do.

3. The exercises should result in the making of a useful article from the very outset; that is to say, an article the use of which is appreciated by the child. This arouses and sustains the child's interest in his work, helps him to understand the reason for every step; for he can see to what these steps lead. It makes him careful in his work, for he soon learns that poor work will spoil a model which he values. The child's self-respect and pride are also aroused: he is not only learning to make, but is actually making. He has joined the army of producers, and he has before him tangible proofs of his progress. If the child is encouraged to make these things for others, it helps, also, to develop unselfishness. Much of the moral value of Sloyd centres in this "useful" model. Some persons, ignorant of its true purpose, have thought it owed its place in this system to its industrial value only. But the truth is that the useful model is valued above all for the mental and moral development secured by use of the creative faculty.

4. Sloyd seeks also to cultivate the æsthetic sense by combining in the models good form and proportion with utility. It has been said by one interested in manual training that "the pupil must be led to see and feel the simple beauty of proportion, of harmony of parts, as well as grace of outline,— elements of beauty which are a direct outgrowth of the useful as well as the beauty of mere ornament which is sometimes more or less externally added. For this reason Sloyd attaches much importance to the free-hand modelling in wood of solid forms." Throughout this system, as in the kindergarten, the sense of beauty is regarded as an important factor in education; and an eye for symmetry and grace, although but rarely developed, has also proved to have great practical value even for the artisan.

5. Every model should be so constructed that it can be drawn by the pupils themselves, not copied or traced. Drawing is an essential feature of Sloyd as applied in Boston, and should always be preliminary to the making of the model.

6. For children who are old enough for the regular Sloyd, it is believed that the knife should be the first and fundamental tool. There are several reasons for this, which will be mentioned later.

These are some of the ideas which have served to guide the arrangement of the models which I have the honor of showing in Chicago. It should be mentioned that Sloyd models are always to be adapted to the needs of different localities.

A radical difference between the Russian and the Swedish system is that the Russian methods are based upon the idea of teaching the use of certain tools by making incomplete articles or exercises, with the belief that out of such teaching will come good educational results, even without much attention to the special needs and capacity of the growing child, either by the choice or the sequence of tools or exercises.

The Swedish system is based upon the Fröbelian idea of the harmonious development of *all* the powers of the child, tools and exercises being chosen with reference to this end, and all merely mechanical methods being carefully avoided. The Sloyd teacher does not say, "Now I will teach this boy to saw, and he shall continue to saw until he can saw well," regardless of monotony or the too prolonged use of the same muscles. The problem of the Sloyd teacher is to find the tool, whether knife or saw or plane, and also the series of exercises, best adapted to the present need of the average pupil, and also to vary or alternate the tools and to graduate the exercises with constant reference to the growing capacity, the formative age, and to the various activities of body and mind.

It should be said here that, while the methods of Sloyd are unlike those aiming at immediate technical skill,— there is abundant proof that the *results* of a thorough Sloyd training will be found to include all that is gained even mechanically by any other method I have seen presented, *plus a far more generous general* development, including greater delicacy of observation and of manipulation. The Sloyd course now being used in Boston calls for the use of forty-five different tools and seventy-two exercises applied in the making of thirty-one models. Among these exercises are fifteen different joints.

Another difference is seen in the importance which Sloyd attaches to the use of the knife as the first tool given to the child, regarding it as the simplest and least mechanical of tools, which gives a development of the muscles of hand and wrist peculiar to itself, a development which modern physiologists teach us is also conducive to the *physical development of the brain,* the familiarity of the tool as well as its danger making it possible to secure concentration of attention upon the work at the outset.

Again, Sloyd methods are unlike Russian methods in giving great prominence to *form study* and in the method by which all form work is made,— methods which are quite unlike those of the carpenter, because the first care of the Sloyd teacher is that the muscular sense of form be developed in the child rather than that the curves be accomplished in the quickest and easiest way.

Again, the exercises of Sloyd furnish greater variety than those of the Russian system; and the fact that small models can be finished in a reasonably short space of time helps to increase and maintain a healthy interest and to train that sense of completeness and achievement, which is unfortunately wanting in many educational processes.

Again, Sloyd methods provide more carefully than is true of some others for the physical development by a judicious choice and sequence of tools, positions, and exercises.

Finally, and most prominent of all differences between the systems, is the insistence of Sloyd upon the use of the *completed model* in place of the prevalent Russian exercise with tools. The reasons for this faith in the educational value of the completed, useful model are similar to those which have so influenced modern pedagogical methods in other departments of education that the completed phrase has now driven the word-spelling out of school and the writing lesson is no longer confined to the copy-book.

Sloyd demands a trained teacher. It is easily seen that the successful carrying out of these ideas depends upon the teacher's comprehension of the object of the teaching and of the capacity and needs of the child, as well as upon his ability to impart the knowledge he has acquired. A good teacher is not necessarily possessed of the manual skill of an expert, but he must understand childish intelligence, and know how to lead the child in his work. I am happy to state that a large number of Boston teachers are now (1893) studying the subject of manual training, and that over ninety-five are taking a normal course in Sloyd.

It is not always enough that a child should be told how to use a tool. The teacher must oversee the work of each child, to make sure that he has a clear idea of what he has to do. Sloyd puts much emphasis on the value of individual instruction; but it must not be supposed that by individual instruction is meant a constant watchfulness of each pupil, much less that the teacher shall take the work into his own hands and give the pupil too much help. A good teacher will not teach too much, even if he has but one pupil. Class instruction can be given as regards much of the manual work,— drawing, positions at the bench, the use, adjustment, and care of tools, etc.; but the best results of Sloyd will not be attained unless a teacher is able also to oversee individual work enough to satisfy himself that his pupil has a clear idea of what he is to do, that he understands the reasons for it, and is not working without thought, mechanically following half-understood directions, and so losing the intellectual value of the exercises. To do this, it will be seen that classes must not be too large. Allowance must be made for difference in physical and mental capacity. It is no matter if two-thirds of the class are in advance of the other third, provided that each pupil receive as much as he can digest. This is not a lesson in memorizing, a test of which is easily applied: here is an attempt to appeal to the perception, the judgment, the ingenuity, the reason, by means of the hand and eye, the *visible* results of which may be good, while the unseen object *of it all is unattained*. Special individual care, therefore, is necessary to make sure that the intellectual development of the child is secured; and teachers must be constantly warned against the *danger of satisfaction with mere manual skill.*

True Sloyd is taught only when, by the exercise of many faculties, the mind is led step by step to careful and accurate thinking.

Sloyd, like the kindergarten, has suffered much from inadequate presentation; and the public have been made more or less familiar with its outward form while wholly ignorant of the aims and psychological basis of its methods. It is for this reason that, while a certain number of persons are always to be found who are attached to the Sloyd models merely because they are useful, others equally unthinking are suspicious of the same models because they are not those of the carpenter shop. Neither of these classes of persons is in a position to do justice to the subject, because neither of them understands the aim of the system or the significance of the exercises embodied in the models, each one of which holds its place in a progressive course of work for a definite reason and as an essential step in the ladder. It will be seen that, although Sloyd models may be adapted to the differing needs of times and places, they must not be taken bodily out of the course, transported, and even arbitrarily combined with other systems and methods, whereby they lose their educational value. It is by such rough handling of its outward symbols that Sloyd has suffered as its mother, the kindergarten, did before it. Let us hope that a better understanding of its methods and of the principles upon which they rest may commend it to students of the philosophy of education.

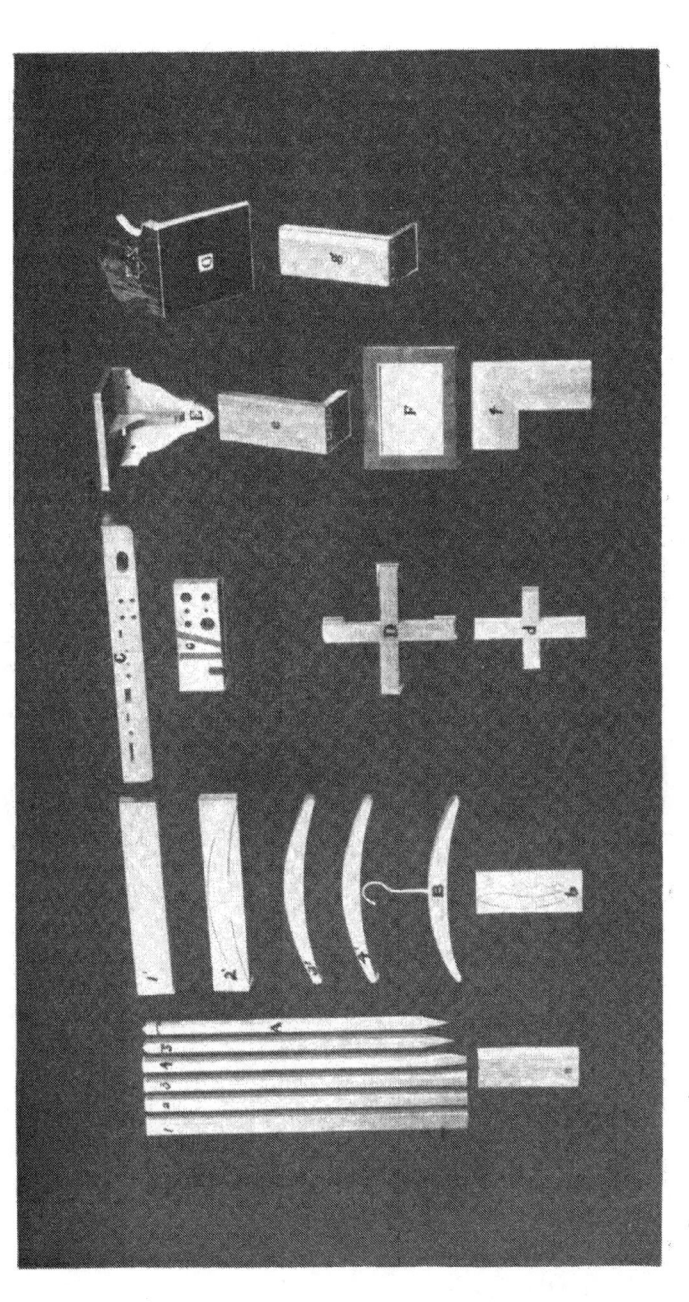

A, B, C, D, E, F, G.—Some High-school Models in Sloyd involving Certain Typical Exercises.—a, b, c, d, e, f, g.—The Same Typical Exercises usually given in the "Russian System" of Manual Training. Models A and B illustrate the Completed Evolution of the Garden-stick and the Coat-hanger.

III.

SLOYD AS A MEANS OF GENERAL EDUCATION.

Paper read at a meeting of the California State Teachers' Asociation in Stockton, Dec. 26, 1893.

It is a great pleasure to me to visit this part of the country, and have the opportunity of explaining to you something of that form of educational manual training known as Sloyd.

The word "Sloyd," pronounced in Swedish "Slöjd," is derived from an old adjective "Slög," meaning skilful. It was used in the writings of the fourteenth century, and always embodied the idea of planning and executing, and was applied to works of art, architecture, embroidery, etc.

The word "Slöjd" has a long history, but this throws very little light on the subject of educational manual training. The word expresses the idea of *planning* and *executing;* and, as it has no equivalent in any language, it seems desirable to adopt it, as the word "Kindergarten" has been adopted. In order to obtain an understanding of the real meaning of the Sloyd system, one must first appreciate the aim of the work and the principles governing the system. Casual observers (and we are sorry that teachers have been found among them) have judged the Sloyd by its outward expression,— *i.e.*, the articles made,— and have never gotten behind them to the vital fact that its value can only be estimated when one has a true knowledge of the needs of childhood, and how this work is arranged to meet these. I need not detain you with a discussion of general principles, but will proceed at once to consider the most important principles governing the Sloyd. I will endeavor to show you how carefully the steps are taken according to educational principles. The physical and mental capacity of the child is first considered, and suitable provision is made for his putting forth the necessary effort to reach an end which he sees and desires. This careful provision is found in the progressive exercises. An exercise in Sloyd is a specific use of a tool, involving a certain mental effort. The principle of correct progression has frequently been overlooked in the arrangement of manual training courses. A strict examination of the prevailing systems would prove many of the exercises to be of very little value in developing the child.

By "variety," must not be understood an incessant changing from one exercise to another before the exercise has had time to produce a definite effect upon the child's mind. This is a very delicate point, a vital one,— a point which I have had constantly in mind in working out my series of models, and which I will endeavor to illustrate to you. Each new exercise must be practised only so long and so steadily as to impress upon the child a correct understanding of it. The exercise must be changed for another before it becomes mechanical, calling for less effort. So soon as this happens, the exercise is no longer an adequate means of development

The opportunity for variety which Sloyd affords must be studied closely, such as : —

1. Variety of exercise.
2. Variety in arrangement of exercises.
3. Variety of objects made.
4. Variety of wood used.
5. Variety of physical effort.
6. Variety of intellectual problems.

Sloyd offers occasion for free-hand work or modelling of solid forms. Experience has taught me that work which can be *tested* by instruments only, sometimes designated as qualitative, is not sufficient of itself to make the child independent and ready to rely on his own judgment. By confining the child to that kind of work which he continually tests by instruments, he grows dependent upon the testing tools, and loses the training of eye and touch. This is the reason for placing in a course, objects having curved outlines which cannot be tested by instruments; for by the eye and sense of touch alone must the pupil judge their correctness. Since the principle that the child shall have free-hand work is considered so important in Sloyd, a proper tool for the work must be provided; and, of all tools, a knife, properly constructed, is found to best meet this need, because it is the most familiar, the simplest and least mechanical. This tool makes the pupil from the beginning of his work feel the need of concentrating his thought upon the work in hand. It teaches the child to think before acting. The knife, however, is not the only tool we use in modelling in wood. The plane, spoke shave, gouge, and file are also used in making the various exercises involved in form work.

A distinction must be made between whittling and so-called knife work. In whittling, the child uses his muscles freely in cutting away shavings, whereby his progress is made visible and his judgment is kept alive in every movement. President Hall has called attention to the fact that the large groups of muscles controlling arms and trunk should be trained before the fine muscles of wrist, hand, and fingers. This makes a sharp distinction between knife work as often practised and whittling. "Knife work," as practised in some systems of manual training, is mostly drawing certain outline forms on wood with the point of a knife, trimming the edges of thin wood to pattern. Thus the knife is reduced to a mere mechanical tool, employed in producing the model, it is true, but affording the child very little opportunity for development. The same is true of the fret-saw. The muscular movement is cramped, and the position is by no means conducive to health; and yet such work has unfortunately come to be called "Educational Manual Training."

Furthermore, Sloyd employs the making and using of

working drawings as a means of concise thought expression; and, therefore, the pupils should make a working drawing of the model before he begins to reproduce it. In most cases the drawing should be made by the pupil himself. However, a drawing not made by the pupil and with which he is not familiar should sometimes be used instead of his own, in order to teach him how to read the thoughts of others. A working drawing represents the object as it *is*, and not as it *looks*.

Sloyd cultivates the æsthetic sense. The pupil is led to see and feel the simple beauty of proportion, of harmony of parts as well as grace of outline,— those elements of beauty which should be found in the useful as well as in the merely ornamental. This is another reason why Sloyd attaches so much importance to the free-hand modelling in wood of solid forms.

Every model should be of good form and proportion.

Sloyd work is arranged so as to provide for a wholesome proportion between problems of thought and of tool work.

Exercises requiring different thought may be produced by the same tool. Thus it will be seen that a rational system of manual training cannot be based upon the tools alone, but on the exercises or the different problems to be worked out by the tool. For example, in planing, the attention is exercised in different ways when planing with the grain and across the grain, though the action of the plane is very similar.

Sloyd offers sufficient opportunity for the cultivation of habits of accuracy by the use of testing instruments, such as rule and try square, and of thorough honesty by the pupil's correction of his own mistakes.

There is hardly another subject in the whole school course which offers such opportunity for the cultivation of habits of rectitude and honesty, or for the prevention of self-indulgence and self-deception, as is afforded by the use of these never-changing, never doubted testing tools, the ruler and try-square. These two tools have been spoken of as emblems of moral rectitude by which the child is led to see and feel what is really honest or straight.

It is an interesting observation, which every teacher of Sloyd can make with his beginners, that the pupils will at first consider their work very good even if it varies one-eighth of an inch, and that it will be but a short time before they have grown critical enough to feel dissatisfied at an error of only one-sixteenth of an inch. And thus the standard of strict honesty will rise, increasing in clearness all the time. In the drawing which the pupil follows, the dimensions of all the parts are given; and a model is not considered correct unless it corresponds exactly with this standard.

Another help to the development of thoroughness, honesty, and truth, is that Sloyd models are finished inside and outside with equal nicety.

In order to assist the child in thus impartially judging his work, some teachers have the pupils write upon their finished work the dimensions they should have obtained and also those they actually have.

Sloyd pays special attention to physical development, and excludes all harmful attitudes and movements; for the child develops rapidly, especially in those muscles and in that direction in which he is most active. Some writers have said that the child will instinctively take the correct working position, but a little observation will show that he may not. However, an enforced position should not always be insisted upon. A few suggestions from the teacher will usually be sufficient to convince the pupil.

Experiments have been made in Sloyd aiming at the equal development of the right and left hand; but as yet it has not been found to be practical, though we still insist upon the use of certain tools with either hand,— namely, saws, planes, bits, etc.

It must not be supposed that Sloyd can take the place

of Educational Gymnastics, or Educational Gymnastics the place of Sloyd, although both aim at general education. There is no conflict between the two: they ought to supplement each other.

It was originally stated that Sloyd was only adapted to small classes or to individual instruction, and all ideal instruction ought to be such. But, since Sloyd is needed for all children of certain grades in public schools, we have to do the best we can with large classes. I should recommend, however, that the maximum number for one teacher be twenty. Since the Sloyd course is so thoroughly graded, it is as well, and better adapted to class instruction than any other course of manual training; for all these kinds of manual training require that some individual attention be given to the pupils. For classes of twenty to thirty pupils it may be necessary to keep the whole class together on the first models. But this working together must not continue beyond the time when the pupils can be effectually handled individually.

It is frequently imagined that Sloyd signifies only a certain set of useful articles, or that it is advocated for its industrial value or for the amusement which it affords the child. Both these conceptions are erroneous. The question of the "useful model" has been carefully considered from a psychological point of view. The child must work for an end that is good and desirable to him, and not merely so to those who are guiding him; for the training of the will depends on "the ideas of the end of the action and by a *vivid feeling* of the *worth* of that end." A child cannot have "a vivid feeling of the worth" of articles that are of no use when completed.

The model is selected by the teacher with a view to the steps to be taken. It must be adapted to the age and condition of the child and to the needs or requirements of the locality where the school is established.

In the Sloyd models which I have the pleasure of presenting here there are required in the actual course of carrying them out seventy-two exercises applied in thirty-one models and executed by forty-seven different tools. "Every model in Sloyd is based upon the exercises of the previous models, and is itself an introduction to the models which are to follow. It is therefore not possible to get a properly arranged course by annexing to a series of joints a few of the most striking Sloyd models. Such a collection of exercises and joints does not, as has been claimed, combine the advantages of both systems. "As it would be futile to extract a single chapter in a novel, apart from the context, and to introduce it into another story, so it is equally meaningless to pick out a few of the Sloyd models, and put them into another wholly different system." Executing abstract exercises, or making miniature parts instead of complete articles, is commonly called the "Russian System of Manual Training." The Russian system is, by the way, not used at all in the public schools of Russia, where they have for years been teaching the Swedish Sloyd. The system of making only parts of things and single joints, commonly adopted in manual training schools in this country, is now confined in Russia to technical institutes, more particularly to the railroad schools, which are special trade-schools. Comparison has often been made between the Russian system and that of Sloyd, saying that "the Russian system made parts and that Sloyd made whole things." But how it could be possible to make whole things without making its parts, also, none of the advocates of the Russian system have ever attempted to demonstrate. In a word, Sloyd, in producing well-made wholes, cannot, of course, slight the parts. But these parts are not kept by themselves, isolated, and therefore hardly comprehensible to the child. They are made with the clear conception that they are indispensable parts of the whole. Therefore, this mode of making parts will be more effective educationally. "No idea or fact is fully comprehended by the pupil until it is made his own, and until he can use it and express it." As the exercises embodied in the useful model of the Sloyd series are based upon pedagogical principles, so the teaching of them must be. Therefore, Sloyd requires a trained teacher; and you will readily see that the average artisan is not likely to bring to the work the required pedagogical insight. Such insight forms the foundation of the work of the teacher, and the combination of this insight with the knowledge of the use of tools constitutes the true Sloyd teacher. The best Sloyd teacher is one who has been thoroughly acquainted with school work, practically as well as theoretically, and who has taken a complete course in Sloyd training. His manual dexterity need by no means be equal to that of an expert mechanic. It is sufficient for him to understand and handle tools, understand the reasons for the exercise, execute exact work, and to direct and supervise the work of his pupils.

In my experience I find that it requires about five hours work daily for five months, for a person who is already a teacher to satisfactorily complete a Sloyd course.

The value of a series of Sloyd models can only be logically tested by a consideration of their fidelity to the fundamental principles of education; capricious changes of models must therefore be regarded with suspicion. It is also evident that, while no one series of models need be arbitrarily used, all adaptations which conform to the same principles will possess strong points of resemblance. So long as the criticism of the complete object forms the basis of judgment, there will be as many systems as there are persons to make new models, and the educational value of manual training will suffer. Not until the motive and the significance of the progression of exercises is understood can the value of any system of work be estimated.

IV.

A FEW FACTS CONCERNING THE WORK OF THE SLOYD TRAINING SCHOOL, BOSTON.

Presented at the graduating exercises, May 25, 1895.

Feeling sure that your interest embraces the whole field of manual training, I believe that you will welcome a brief report from that corner of the field committed to my care.

There are certain misapprehensions regarding our work which I would like to correct. One is that Sloyd methods do not provide for sufficient practice with tools. In this connection let me say that the Sloyd Training School is just issuing some pamphlets, which, I hope, will receive your attention.

In the charts accompanying these pamphlets I have emphasized a feature of Sloyd that is not always appreciated. This is the *repetition* of exercises which Sloyd affords, and which is not always properly attended to by the teachers.

I think I have succeeded in showing on these new charts, not only the new exercises in each model, but the very frequent *repetition* of exercises, resulting in the acquirement of skill, without monotony, which has hitherto failed of recognition.

Another mistaken notion about Sloyd is that it is regarded as a finished, perfect system by its promoters. I can speak with some authority in this matter, and I deprecate most earnestly any idea of finality in *this* as in any other branch of educational work. Sloyd stands for *study*, for *growth*, and for *progress*. There is nothing fixed or final about it.

The models and exercises used to-day we are ready to

set aside to-morrow for something better; and I want to report that this has just been done with our elementary course, in which nine models have been replaced by such as seemed better suited to our purpose.

The only thing about our work which I regard as a fixed fact is that the basis is sound, that we are "headed" in the right direction; and my confidence is strengthened by many unexpected letters of encouragement and commendation which I have received during the past year from eminent educators, and scholars in various parts of the United States, particularly by those from leading psychologists. Another and more practical test of the aim of our work is the result obtained by Sloyd methods in places where it has had abundant opportunity to show its possibilities, as, for instance, in the work of the Concord Reformatory and the Lyman School, Westboro, where Sloyd has been for the past few years a daily exercise; and where the leading officers of those institutions, having a rare opportunity to observe its mental and moral influence, declare it to be greater than that of any reformatory agent which has come under their observation. The manual skill derived from it has been more than satisfactory. It is particularly significant that in those institutions industrial work of various kinds has long been carried on, and can now be seen side by side with the Sloyd.

It is gratifying to announce that more than ten thousand children in the United States are receiving instruction in Sloyd given by graduates of our training classes, of whom we have sent out fifty-five. Two hundred and forty-three teachers have been enrolled in the Sloyd Training School, and over one hundred have been in attendance during the past year (1895).

I have recently spent much time in investigating the work in manual training in high schools. I have watched classes at work in various places, and have talked freely with teachers and directors. I am happy to report that I find men of established reputation engaged in this work, who do not consider the present methods as final, and who feel, as I do, that there is possibility as well as need of improvement in these courses. This fact and the recent act of the legislature of Massachusetts, requiring manual training in high schools in every city having over twenty thousand inhabitants, has decided me to devote my summer this year to the effort of working out and arranging a high-school course in accordance with the broadest educational principles.

In undertaking this work, I shall warmly welcome the co-operation of men of experience everywhere who agree with me that the manual training methods of the future must be kept abreast of and in harmony with the best educational methods of the day, and that if we, who now occupy the field, do not meet the demand of the times, there are those just ahead of us in the moral and intellectual fields of work who will surely and shortly supersede us.

A course of manual training for high schools must teach the correct use of the various tools in such constructive work as embodies the underlying principles of the mechanic arts, and in such a way that the pupil may gain the utmost *general power* attainable through the acquisition of manual skill.

The course I have in mind will cover a period of three years in the high school, and consists of bench-work, wood-turning, and wood-carving in connection with mechanical drawing.

I ask your attention to points which I consider basal in any course of work for manual training in high schools.

1. The course should be based upon progressive exercises, and not upon models or tools, the progression being in accordance with the growing power of the worker.*

2. Every exercise should be such as to give the pupil a good reason, from his point of view, for putting forth his best effort.

---
* By an exercise in Sloyd I mean a specific use of a tool involving certain mental and physical effort. Rational progression will hardly allow *more* than four or *less* than one new exercise in a model.

3. The exercises should be applied on *objects* the use of which can be thoroughly appreciated by the pupil.

4. Preference should be given to exercises which will aid the pupil in the laboratory or other school work.

5. Every piece of work should be, if possible, of truly artistic form and proportion.

6. The course should be interspersed with work which develops appreciation of curves and the exercise of the sense of form and touch in judging the correctness.

7. Working drawings based and executed on scientific principles should precede the making of each object.

8. Tools and instruments should be such as are in general use; and preference should be given to those which aid physical development and which are the least mechanical, with a view to the fullest development of the worker's original power.

9. All practice given *merely* for the sake of gaining facility in the use of tools should be avoided.

10. A variety of common native wood suited to the character of the objects should be used and studied.

Firmly believing that the efficiency of this training is not limited to any particular line of work, and that it should accomplish nothing less than real "fitting for life," the making of true citizens, I urge the importance of placing work which holds such possibilities in the hands of *true teachers*.

Whoever teaches manual training must of course be skilled in the mechanic arts; but, if he has not pedagogical tact, if he cannot touch the springs of action in the life of youth so that the best is brought into full play, I do not care very much to know that he has exceptional technical skill in any special line of work. What I do want to know is that he is first and foremost an earnest student of the life of youth, and that he works to promote its healthful growth. *Rightly directed power* is what we are after, and the acquisition of certain skill must be made a means to this end. A true teacher knows how to use this means so that the forces for good become dominant in the life.

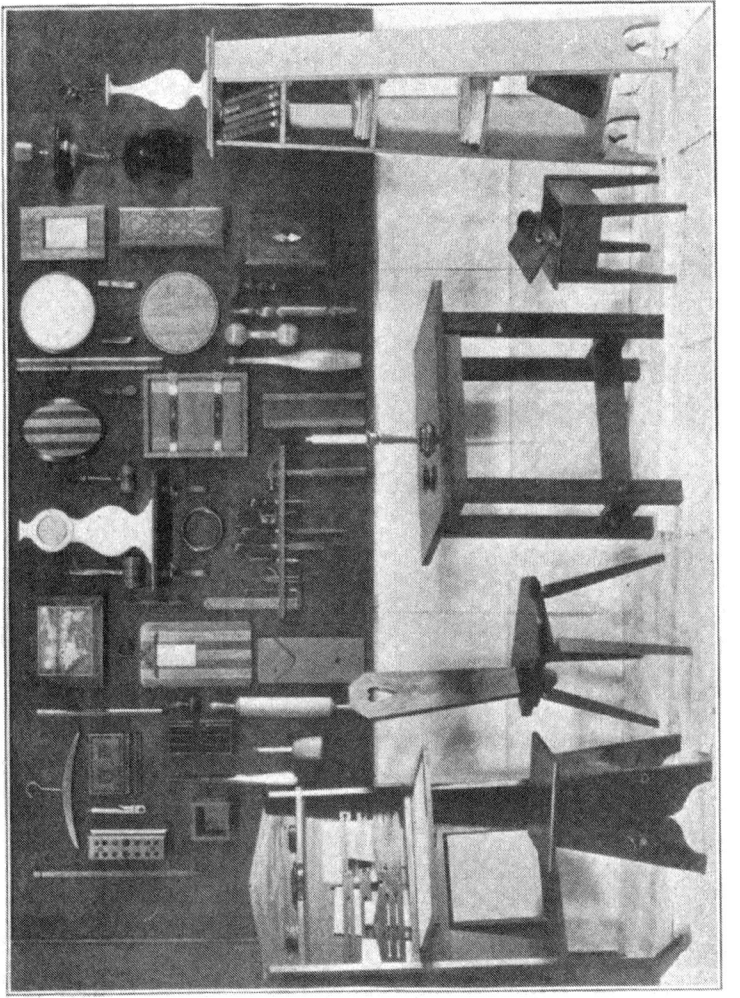

SLOYD FOR HIGH SCHOOLS.

V.

SLOYD.

Address delivered, at the invitation of the Connecticut State Teachers' Association, at New Haven, Oct. 16, 1896.

As I am an advocate of manual training, you doubtless think of me as an enthusiastic specialist, who sees in manual training a remedy for all the failings of the schools; and you perhaps expect me to offer a few arbitrary, technical methods for your consideration, with which to effect reforms. Allow me to say from the outset that my mission is not that of a specialist who fails to appreciate the value of all educational influences except his own special cure-all. I have not, and never expect to have, any cast-iron methods of manual training to recommend. My work is, however, a constant effort to discover the largest possibilities of manual training as a factor in general education. It is not unlike the work to which each one of you is devoted. I ask you, therefore, to listen, not as to one who has merely a new, outside subject to urge upon the schools, but to one who is working with you for the best means of developing character in the children committed to our charge. This, and only this, I believe, should be the test of all subjects taught in public schools; and should it not also be the guide in the choice of methods by which all educational work is carried on?

Our school courses are already overcrowded, and the expense of carrying on the schools is already great. We are, therefore, not justified in introducing a new subject, unless a careful study of the growing child convinces us that his welfare demands it; and then it becomes an absolute necessity. The chief value of that form of manual training which I shall endeavor to present to you is not that it will directly help children to earn their living, fit them for a trade, or discover to them their professional bent. These are good aims and ends, which ought to be accomplished, and which will be furthered by the means I shall recommend; but they are not the real purpose of general education, nor are they the special business of the public schools. What is the aim of education? This is the question that teachers and promoters of special movements should constantly ask themselves. Is it not the development of good mental habits, power in active doing, and the healthy and happy life? That is my idea of its mission, and I believe that I only share the feeling of our best educators. A recent writer in the *Educational Review* says, "Without our knowing it, the social ideal of an intelligent, full, free, happy human life for every boy and girl born or brought into our midst has gained possession of our minds and hearts." Dr. C. Hanford Henderson, in the *Popular Science Monthly*, also says, "What we want is radiant boys, breathing the full breath of life and health, thinking clearly, feeling deeply, rich in the fine riches of the human spirit,— the riches that come from the expanding and unfolding of the human faculties."

This is the spirit of the times, or, rather, it is the spirit of true teaching. It is the spirit that possessed Comenius, Pestalozzi, Fröbel, and the spirit that has possessed all true teachers. Let it possess us and guide us. Let it control whatever means we employ, whatever we carry into the school. The end will control the means used to secure it. The end, as we see it, demands a sound body, controlled by an intelligent mind, and a free, joyous spirit. We who undertake manual training must consider, then, how to promote and employ physical power most effectively; and, to do this, I think that we must make the spontaneous interests of childhood the basis of sustained effort. If such consideration were foremost with every manual training teacher, if the natural interests and development of childhood rather than the acquirement of technical skill were to determine the courses of manual work planned for children, there would be a revolution in many manual training schools. I should never expect all manual training teachers to use exactly the same methods or the same courses of work; but the principles of education are universal, and, wherever these are followed, there will be a certain similarity of methods. For instance, could a teacher who is alive to the value of the spontaneous interests of boyhood put a boy to work on abstract exercises for which he can see no use? If the manual training teacher appreciates the importance of a normal physical growth, would he fail to provide for it, or would he allow such work or the use of such tools as retard or interfere with that growth, however fascinating the work might be? Let me take, for example, the much-advocated and much-used fret-saw and the knife work in thin wood, both of which are commonly used in a sitting position, with constant repetition of the same movements, giving no general physical development, and even tending sometimes to injurious bodily results. The argument that children like it is hardly sufficient to justify its use. Amusement is often mistaken for interest. It is not safe to argue that what fascinates a child is always desirable for him. The problem is to make attractive that which is desirable. When I was a boy, we used to be exceedingly amused by standing on our heads and seeing which could eat the most candy in that position; but the mental or physical benefit of the exercise might be reasonably questioned. Only the other day I met a manual training teacher who told me that he had taken a course in elementary manual work during the summer. He considered it "excellent" on account of the many attractive objects he had made and the problems he had worked out; but he said that his muscles ached from the continuous, one-sided, cramped movements required for the work. It seems needless to say that such manual training as this, whether popular or not, should be condemned. When a child is set to sawing, and made to continue that exercise until he has mastered sawing, then planing until he can do skilful planing, or, indeed, if he be kept too long at any continuous and monotonous exercise, then it is certain that even the physical needs of the worker have not been taken into account. But this is not all: we should also ask ourselves what the boy is thinking about while he is sawing, planing, etc. Has he been doing work which gratifies the taste, which trains the eye to see beauty of line, form, and proportion, and which awakens natural enthusiasm? In short, has his life been touched, at as many points as possible, through the work he has in hand? The amount of hand-work accomplished, the ability to saw and plane exactly or to make a few joints correctly, is not what we are now after. The mind and heart of the boy must not be forgotten while his hands are supplied with work. Psychologists tell us that skill does not exist in the hand, but in the brain. Let the work, then, appeal to the intelligence of the worker. Let it require his full thought and attention, cultivate his taste, and, above all, let it, as far as possible, appeal to the human heart. Let what he makes be something, if possible, connected with the most natural and best interests of his life, so that, while his hands are at work, his thoughts are likely to be wholesome, generous, and joyous. In the words of another, "Let the boy in the manual training school get the satisfaction out of his work which the boy on the farm feels when allowed to help shingle the shed, which the girl feels when she makes her first loaf of bread or sets the last stitch in a finished garment; for by such simple methods, which are God's own ways, is developed that moral enthusiasm the lack of which is said to be the crying need of our public education."

If you think that manual skill, as such, will necessarily make our children better, consider the great skill and intelligence of those who pick locks and construct infernal machines. Reflect a moment upon the skill of many inmates of our prisons and reformatories. How have they acquired it? Often, I believe, by laborious practice to obtain accuracy and skill of hand, with no other conscious motive than the attainment of that skill. This is to me a very important point. Believing, as I do, that habits and ideas which are formed during vigorous muscular effort are the most impressive and lasting, it is my opinion that the motive of the worker, whether near or remote, should be seriously considered in every step of manual training; and a satisfactory motive is best supplied, I think, in the production of useful objects for the worker himself, his home, or his friends, objects also which furnish the pleasantest and most wholesome association of ideas. By this you will see that it will not be possible or rational to have a fixed set of objects for every country or school: the worker, his tastes, needs, and surroundings, must always be kept in mind. As manual training comprises all hand-work, it is to be considered what material is best fitted for school purposes. We should choose such as will give *the greatest variety* of healthful, vigorous physical movements; and, among all occupations tried, working in wood with a large variety of carpenters' tools has been found best for this purpose. Wood is clean, also; and the work-room should be clean and orderly, like a school, and not like a shop. The system of wood-work which seems to me most nearly to fulfil the desired conditions is called Sloyd. What is Sloyd? It is not knife work wholly or chiefly. Sloyd is not a set of models. It is not a prescribed course of exercises. It is not the use of certain tools. Sloyd is a system of educational hand-work, so arranged and carried out as to employ and direct the vigorous self-activity of a student for a purpose which he recognizes as good. The spontaneous exercise of the creative faculty for a useful and good end is a moral tonic. The mere acquisition of skill is not necessarily so. It will be seen that, when a manual training teacher says that he has "partly Sloyd" and partly some other system, it is the same as to say, "Partly I provide for what is best for the child, and partly I do something else." Such work cannot be based on sound educational principles; neither can that where models are used without appreciation of their significance, although this is sometimes called Sloyd. It is no wonder that earnest investigators of systems of manual training are confused by the cries of "Lo here! and lo there!" If there are such in my audience, let me advise them to put a few searching questions before they pass judgment upon any course of work. These questions will show what the Sloyd standard is, and will help to determine when a given course of work may properly bear that name.

1. Are the models useful, serviceable objects, which are likely to arouse the lively interest of young pupils?

2. Are the exercises and tools arranged with reference to the worker's growth of power? Do they call for a gradual increase of effort, step by step?

3. Does the first exercise with each tool give a correct, effective impression of its typical use?

4. Do the objects afford due variety of form, and are the proportions good?

5. Are curved outlines, to which ordinary testing tools cannot be applied, conspicuous thoughout the course?

6. Do the finished models represent, in every respect, the pupil's own work?

7. Are tools and exercises selected with reference to physical development?

I hope you will not infer from anything I have said that I do not value manual skill in teacher and in pupil. I have only tried to show that skill is not the primary consideration. It has been truly said of general education that, "where technical results are given first consideration, there the largest possibilities of educational work must always be seriously dwarfed or lost altogether," and also that "technical skill must be taught its place in manual training as in other branches of education." I, for one, firmly believe that here as elsewhere, while skill is not undervalued, it must be regarded as subservient to that which is the highest aim of all training, a broad and noble manhood and womanhood. These are ambitious words, but I believe that manual trainers must not be more willing than other teachers to accept a lower aim. As a matter of fact, manual training, based upon the principles which I have tried to set before you, when well taught, under favorable conditions, will in the end insure a higher degree of general skill than is attainable by the more technical or industrial methods. Striking examples of this may be found in certain places where Sloyd is used side by side with the trade-school. Of course, the manual training teacher should have a very considerable degree of manual skill and a thorough knowledge of the technical part of the subject; but a mechanic or draftsman cannot often be safely employed as a teacher on account of his technical skill alone or chiefly. Long experience in using carpenters' tools and draftsmen's instruments does not necessarily fit one for this work. Psychological insight and the teacher's training and tact are of first importance here as elsewhere; and, if we can add to these a high degree of technical skill, we shall have an ideal manual training teacher. Such a combination, however, is rare; and, of the two, the teacher is to be preferred to the mechanic for manual training every time. It is safer to have a person who is three-quarters teacher and one-quarter mechanic than the reverse.

It is my experience that about one year of special training in manual training work will fit one who is already a good teacher to conduct the tool work in grammar schools. For high-school work additional time would be necessary.

A few words about the material part of the work. Large, well-lighted, and well-ventilated rooms should always be provided for manual training. For many reasons it is a great mistake to put this work into inferior rooms. It is not only unhygienic, but the whole subject is then likely to be looked upon as merely an appendix to the school, and to be less respected by both teacher and pupil. As for basements or rooms not perfect in sanitary conditions, they should not be considered for a moment. The best order should prevail. Tools and materials should be kept on neatly arranged shelves and racks, all, if possible, within sight. The best quality of tools should be selected: they are the cheapest in the long run. A fine finish of shelves, benches, and racks, is recommended, as securing greater care. Rough benches and tools are often found to be scratched and cut. The price of a manual training outfit varies according to the number and quality of tools used. The grammar schools in the cities I am acquainted with have usually estimated the cost at about $20 for each child. This outfit is quite complete and of the best quality. An ordinary school-room, 28 x 32 feet, will conveniently accommodate twenty pupils, which number I consider large enough for one teacher to handle satisfactorily. Running expenses for material, such as wood and paper, are comparatively slight, about seventy-five cents a year for each child.

VI.

SOME OBSERVATIONS ON MANUAL TRAINING IN EUROPE AND AMERICA.

Paper read at the meeting of the Committee on Manual Training of the New England Educational Workers, Nov. 11, 1896.

I have been honored by being asked to speak about manual training as I have observed it in this country and in Europe. These observations are necessarily colored by my own convictions. I have noticed that, wherever a free silver advocate travelled, he found the people unanimously in favor of free silver; while a sound money advocate, visiting the same region, found overwhelming majorities in favor of the gold standard.

A manual training teacher may visit a country, and return with enthusiastic accounts of what he found there, because the work he saw accorded with his own notions; while another, visiting the same country, will condemn the methods used. Mere statistics, of course, are not affected by individual views; but I know your interest is not confined to bare facts. You are bristling with whys and wherefores.

I want to take a few moments to explain to you the standpoint from which I view this matter of manual training. I am particularly anxious to make this clear because I fear that I have not always been successful in the past in this respect. I fear that I have sometimes failed to make my position understood, even by those who have been closely associated with me in this work.

I do not ask you to attend to me because I have travelled somewhat, and have visited many schools. Emerson tells us that " travelling is a symptom of unsoundness, affecting the whole intellectual action," that "they who made England, Italy, or Greece venerable in the imagination, did so by sticking fast where they were." What he says in this connection of the artist who seeks foreign cities in order to make an artist of himself seems to me applicable to the teacher who thinks it necessary to go abroad to acquire the teacher's spirit. I shall take the liberty of substituting the word "teacher" for "artist" in the sentence of Emerson which I am about to quote: "It was in his own mind that the teacher sought his model." "It was an application of his own thought to the thing to be done and the conditions to be observed." "Beauty, convenience, grandeur of thought, are as near to us as to any; and if the American teacher will study with hope and love the precise thing to be done by him, considering the climate, the soil, the length of the day, the wants of the people, the habit and form of government," then, I would say, the purpose of education will be fulfilled. Do not think, however, that I do not also appreciate the benefit of travel and the observation of good work, wherever it is to be found.

But the question is not How much has one seen, how much has one travelled, but What has he looked for, and with what intelligence has he investigated? The purpose in it all is the only thing which should command respect. I want to say from the outset that I advocate manual training only in so far as it furthers to the utmost of its capacity the high purpose of general education. To explain what I mean by that, I would refer all teachers to an article by Dr. Hanford Henderson, entitled "The Aim of Modern Education"; and I ask you to bear in mind that it was written by the principal of one of the leading manual training schools in this country. While I heartily believe in this broad view of education, and feel strongly that the manual training teacher should consider the training of the whole child, I do not claim that manual training is the only remedy for the shortcomings of the schools. I do think, however, that it might be made one of the most effective agents in general education.

As a test of manual training, I have sometimes thought it would be well to imagine a boy who has been most skilfully trained in manual work suddenly deprived of his hands. Then let the teacher ask himself, What has that boy been acquiring which is not lost by this calamity? If it can be shown that by means of this manual work a gain has been made in physical development, the power of clear thinking, strength of character and will power, then one has a right to feel that the most important aim of manual training has been accomplished. And I firmly believe that, where these results are the first consideration, manual skill and ability for bread-winning will be greater than where skill is the chief aim of the work. With this idea in my mind, I have always investigated methods of manual training. I have taken very little pains to gather statistics in my travels. I have not been moved to hasten thither by hearing that some very elaborate models and carvings have been worked out in Holland, or that there is a school in Vienna which teaches fanciful designs in leather and poker drawing; but I believe that I would travel on my hands and knees, if necessary, to find manual training in the hands of a great teacher. I believe that manual training teachers are on the wrong track whenever they try to get at the heart of manual training by seeking the largest establishments and greatest variety of industrial pursuits. I have heard that all that is needed to make a university is a log with Mark Hopkins on one end of it and a student on the other. Perhaps the greatest and most important manual training school that has yet existed was the spot where Cygnæus and Salomon held counsel together. In Finland there were no extensive shops to go through, no great schools to visit, but there was a teacher. I wish I could tell you that I have always found manual training, either in Europe or America, in the hands of teachers; but my observation will show that, on the contrary, this work is still too generally in the hands of mechanics and artisans.

The teachings of Herr Salomon in Sweden are too well known in this company to need comment from me. But even in Sweden, as elsewhere, there is too wide a gulf between theory and practice; and the equipment of the Sloyd schools is still comparatively poor. There are, however, certain advantages there which ought to be taken into consideration. The artisan teachers are becoming fewer and fewer, and only those who have shown teaching ability are now generally retained.

The smaller number of pupils given to each teacher, twenty being the largest number, is a very important feature of the Swedish schools. The regular teacher is trained to teach the Sloyd; and this insures, in the first place, the holding of the teacher's certificate by the manual training instructor, also the better acquaintance with his pupils, which enables him to reach certain individual weaknesses and difficulties through his manual training.

In Gothenburg, Sweden, there are now twenty-five manual training centres, where all the boys in the four upper grammar grades receive instruction in wood-work and some in iron-work. The teachers, according to the rules and regulations, should give forty-four hours instruction a week; but they give at present only forty-two hours, or seven hours a day six days in the week. Each pupil receives from six to eight hours' instruction a week, divided into three lessons. The maximum number of pupils in a class is twenty, and the instruction is almost entirely individual.

Working drawings are used, but not made. They are bound in convenient book form for each pupil. The course is based entirely upon Sloyd principles, though the models differ somewhat from those used at Nääs. It was particularly interesting to watch a class in iron-work. The boys used their tools with remarkable precision and interest. The models of this course are finished, useful articles, all progressively arranged. The teachers hold monthly meetings to discuss matters regarding the instruction, change of models, etc.; and a society formed among the Sloyd teachers owns quite an extensive library of books and pamphlets on education and manual training in particular. In Gothenburg I was glad to see also that Sloyd is used in the high school with marked success. This is rational, for Sloyd is simply manual training adapted to the needs of pupils of any age. The moral gain to boys in making useful objects should not be ignored in high-school work. If acquiring skill were always associated with accomplishing a definite good, which the worker appreciates, idleness and crime would be less frequent in our midst.

At the seventh Scandinavian school meeting, held in Stockholm last year, over six thousand teachers from Sweden, Norway, Denmark, and Finland, were represented. Several papers on manual training were read, followed by full discussion. I also had the pleasure at this meeting of presenting a paper on Sloyd in American schools. At this meeting the following resolution was unanimously adopted: "Manual training in schools must be arranged in accordance with general educational principles." The instruction should consequently : —

1. Begin with concrete objects.

2. Proceed from the easy to the more difficult without break.

3. It should be individual.

4. Should give general development of the pupil's powers, arouse interest in manual work, promote order, exactness, and neatness, develop self-activity, and lastly, which is the chief condition, it should be carried on by a properly trained teacher who has sufficient insight and skill in both theory and practice.

It seems strange that in Germany, the home of so many great educators, manual training should not be greatly practised in the schools. I had some interesting talks with Dr. Goetze. He is the leader of the manual training movement in Germany, and director of the Manual Training Teacher's Institute at Leipzig. He deplores the fact that his country is so slow to see the necessity of this work. He told me that there is a great need in Germany of the philanthropic public spirit, which has done so much in the United States to make the benefits of manual training recognized. In Dr. Goetze's school a great variety of manual work is taught, such as wood-work, clay, cardboard, and metal work. In this school, as at Nääs, there are short courses for teachers which can be taken in a few weeks. With the exception of one or two practice pieces in each course the models are all finished objects. In form and proportion, and also in the progression of exercises, the models seem to me not wholly satisfactory. The cardboard work seems to be very good, particularly in the choice of color and material; but I should consider it to be too difficult for children. The tuition for each course for normal students is seventy-five marks (about eighteen dollars). I found the students very enthusiastic in their work; but the preparation they were making for teaching manual training seemed to me to be inadequate, unless the preliminary training had been very thorough.

The instructors, with the exception of the learned Dr. Goetze, are skilful artisans merely. The German Association for Manual Instruction is doing very effective work in Germany through publications, meetings, and constant agitation of the subject. I met the able president, Herr von Schenckendorff, whose writings I had read for years. I found him very hopeful and enthusiastic. At Halle I visited Franke's famous institutions, and was surprised and disappointed not to find any kind of manual training practised there,— the very subject upon which the famous founder laid so much stress. It will be remembered that August Hermann Franke is the man whose faith in the health-giving power of manual work was so great that he had wood-turning lathes introduced in the children's hospital at Halle, in order to give the children as soon as possible healthy and interesting exercises.

At the Berlin educational exhibit, which I visited last summer, the most conspicuous feature of the manual training department was the chip-carving. This very ornamental and fascinating work I know by experience to be extremely tedious, too much so, I believe, for the good of children.

The interesting exhibit made by the Pestalozzi-Fröbelhaus in Berlin, while far ahead of anything I saw in Germany in that line of manual work, did not seem to me to compare favorably with the kindergarten work done in this country. The exhibit of illustrations and apparatus for science work was most complete and excellent. England seems to be very wide-awake to the importance of manual training. I have met the leading manual training instructors of London, Sheffield, Birmingham, Manchester, and Liverpool, have had some interesting conferences and correspondence with them, and have seen their classes at work. In Sheffield and Manchester, where some trained teachers are employed, Sloyd models are largely used. In London, Liverpool, and Birmingham some practice pieces are used; but these are rapidly going out of favor. With a few exceptions the instructors in these cities were artisans. In Birmingham I met Mr. A. W. Bevis, a leader of manual training, and found him a most interesting example of a skilful engineer, who is also a natural teacher and an eager student. His conferences with the teachers of young children are very interesting and suggestive. I was especially interested in his plan for paper-folding, brick-laying, and parcel-tying, and the drawings connected with these things, all to be carried on in the regular class-room by the class teacher.

During last summer I had a very interesting interview, also, with Mr. A. B. Badger, organizing secretary for technical instruction. He is the notable English teacher who was lately commissioned to investigate and make a report on manual training. He made a thorough investigation and a full report. This report made a careful comparison between the usual practice work with tools and that which is based upon purely educational principles. He pays a high tribute to Sloyd, which has also many other enthusiastic advocates in England. I should say that, in the literature of manual training, England is far ahead of other countries. Large numbers of English teachers go yearly to Nääs to take the course there and get the inspiration of Herr Salomon's lectures. So far as I know, there is in England no special school for fitting teachers for manual training. Short courses of five or six weeks are given, during the summer months, in various parts of the country by private teachers. Examinations for manual training teachers are, however, held under the city and guild of London Institute and other educational bodies. For the advanced certificate of the Educational Handwork Union a record of fifty hours' practical work in a class conducted by an approved teacher is required, besides the writing of a thesis, some drawing, and the making of an original model.

The manual training movement has been more fortunate in this country in many respects than in Europe. Philanthropy has aided it,— indeed, has been its entering wedge, — while the interest and co-operation of American teachers has been of great value to the cause. The buildings, tools, and equipments in America also surpass any I have seen in Europe; and the number of manual training schools increases more rapidly here.

Before we congratulate ourselves, however, upon the rapid multiplication of manual training schools in our midst, it is well to know what these schools are doing.

The school is a good thing when it stands for education;

but a school, however well equipped, in the hands of Dickens's Mr. Squeers, had better not exist. The investigations of your society are just what is needed to show us what manual training schools are and what they should be; and, if my fragmentary observations can aid in this work, I shall be very glad. I have already expressed the thought that the teacher is the first consideration in every manual training school; and, in estimating the worth of a teacher, I do not for a moment wish to undervalue manual skill or the ability to impart information, but I feel strongly that educational reasoning should control his work in practice as well as theory. With this in view, I have carried on my observations; and I have found in too many schools that secondary motives control the work. Let me take a few examples from actual experience.

A teacher of manual training once said to me: "I invented my own system. I change it a little every year as I see fit. I have been working as a foreman in a machine shop for twelve years, so I know just how to do things in the right way. If anybody should copy my exercises, I should change the whole course in twenty-four hours."

If that man were to study the character and ability of his pupils, and base his work upon their individual needs, he would find that his "shop-work" was but a small proportion of what was needed in the make-up of a teacher, and that suitable courses of work cannot be so speedily produced.

Another instructor mentions his graduation from a polytechnic school and his success as a draughtsman. To him, "drawing is the climax of manual training"; and he would spend much time upon it. Is drawing the climax of manual training?

Manual training may develop the power of right action through well-directed movements; and that power so strengthened and developed is, to my mind, the climax of manual training. Drawing, as a means of thought expression, has its place; but it is by no means the climax.

Another teacher says: "This is my method. First give practical exercises with tools, then make a finished object, then a real working drawing from that object." What do you think of that method? Doesn't it put the cart before the horse?

Another says: "I have a system worked out at the school, but I have changed it a little to suit my taste. I use Sloyd for the younger boys and the Russian system for the older ones. I keep my class together to get more uniform work and to spare myself." What do you suppose he means by Sloyd? Should his taste and convenience be first considered, or the needs of his pupils?

Another tells me: "I am an expert in wood-work and drawing. I will guarantee to keep children interested without ever making anything but problems." In this case, is it the problem that arouses the interest or is it the teacher? Another says: "I perform in my class all the exercises before the eyes of my boys, and require them to do exactly what I have done. Then, you see, I have time to give individual instruction." Does not this instructor substitute memory for mind? A teacher of fifteen years' experience gives me the following: "When we are working in pine wood, I spend about one-half hour speaking about pine-trees, their growth, leaves, fruit, etc. I am more of a science teacher than a mechanic, and I will admit that many of the boys do better work than I do." Does this teacher look upon muscular training as an essential part of manual training? and, if so, can he afford to give less than two hours a week to the exercise of muscular activity?

In the most exhaustive report which has been issued upon manual training in America this statement appears from the pen of a well-known leader in this department: "What is known as the 'Russian Method' of tool instruction consists of a series of exercises based upon and accompanied by an analysis of three things,— the tools, the materials, and the elements of construction. If we add to this basis of three things a fourth thing,— namely, the boy himself, his physical and mental condition,— we have the sufficient basis for both the method and the content of American manual training." The instances which I have just cited illustrate Professor Woodward's description of the method and content of American manual training. They show that exercises, tools, drawings, or something of that sort, are made the basis; and the boy, by an afterthought, is added as the last element in the scheme. If these ideas were exactly reversed and the boy put first, I believe there would be a revolution in means and methods in most manual training schools.

VII.

MANUAL TRAINING AS A FACTOR IN PHYSICAL EDUCATION.

Paper read before the Boston Society for the Advancement of Physical Education, Feb. 11, 1897.

It is very gratifying to me to be invited to say a few words to this learned society on the possibilities of manual training as a factor in physical education.

I have devoted many years to the study and teaching of manual training, not with a view to rapidly acquiring skill, but always looking upon it as a branch of general education. I hope that my strong interest in my subject, together with the pictures and tools I have brought with me, will enable me to make my ideas clear to you. I cannot, of course, answer for all the methods of manual training practised in the schools. I shall only speak of my own personal aims and experience, and point out the chief principles governing that form of manual training known as Sloyd. I shall endeavor to show that the promoters of Sloyd have made special provision for promoting healthy physical and mental growth in its arrangement of exercises and in the choice of tools and material. I believe that these facts have not always been understood by the promoters of physical education. As there are many mistaken notions about Sloyd, allow me to state briefly what it stands for and to correct some common misapprehensions on the subject.

"Sloyd is tool work, so arranged and employed as to stimulate vigorous, intelligent self-activity for a purpose which the boy recognizes as good." It is not merely, as some people think, a system of manual training, employing a few small tools for making a certain set of small things particularly adapted for small children. It is a system which makes use of more tools and more exercises than any other course of manual training known to me; and it is adaptable to all grades of schools which aim to give a general education. It is a system not based upon tools or construction or the making of useful articles: it is based upon the needs and demands of the growing child. It is therefore a system which cannot be taught with profit by a mere mechanic or artisan any more than educational gymnastics can be taught by an athlete. Sloyd must be taught by one who understands and appreciates the needs of children and youth, their physical conditions, and their ways of feeling and thinking,— one who is always trying, in fact, to direct muscular and mental activity in such a way as to promote the best health and the best thought. Sloyd is based on the idea that no manual training is educational in its true sense, however profitable and fascinating its results may appear to be, unless it employs and develops physical powers in the right way. Certainly, with such considerations as its guide, manual training should be a help in physical education.

I do not, however, for a moment think that Sloyd can be made to take the place of educational gymnastics; neither can educational gymnastics take the place of Sloyd. We need them both. They are not subjects of rivalry. Educational gymnastics, as I understand it, aims at the symmetrical training of the whole body. Even ideal Sloyd cannot do all this, but its effort is in the same direction; for, unlike some other courses of manual training, it not only excludes such tools and exercises as would have a tendency to interfere with the natural growth, but it must provide in its tool work for free, natural, healthy exercise of the larger muscles, without too much monotony and with carefully graded resistances.

About twelve years ago an experiment was made at Nääs, Sweden, to provide for the fuller developmemt of both sides of the body, by making children work at their Sloyd with the left hand as well as with the right. This might seem correct, from a physiological point of view, and I believe that we should, to some extent, encourage such methods; but to keep this up continuously was found not to be practicable. In the case of such children as have already acquired the right-handed habit, the disappointment of spoiling their tool work, while using the left hand, is too great, and the work is too much interrupted. Much can be, and is done, however, looking to the same result, by as large a use as possible of *tools which employ both hands equally*.

I have during the past ten years discarded a number of models, chiefly on account of too little opportunity afforded for the free natural use of the muscles. By the fundamental principles of Sloyd, labor-saving contrivances and machinery are also practically excluded. The material result obtained by the child should be as far as possible a true representation of his own muscular and mental effort; and this idea has, I think, both a physical and a moral significance.

Another point taken into consideration is the development of touch and sight by introducing models of solid forms with curved outlines, not susceptible of mechanical tests. Some of the methods employed in metal work, the use of the bracket saw, wood-carving, and so-called "knife work" (which is really cutting with a cramped hand instead of free whittling), although convenient work in the school-room, are examples of manual training which give little natural muscular development. Indeed, I consider the effect of some of these exercises positively injurious.

I heartily wish that teachers and promoters of manual training who are satisfied with the methods usually employed might avail themselves of the advice of physical educators, and that a closer co-operation might exist between the promoters of physical and manual training. The latter work would then have such supervision as would give direct help to teachers.

In 1890 I published a "Teacher's Sloyd Manual," calling attention to some of the working positions most important from a hygienic point of view, with directions for the use of tools.

The next year I had an article in one of the school papers, showing the importance of right postures and movements in manual training; but a second illustrated article on the same subject was refused by an editor, who said that he did not think there was much interest in that subject, and yet manual training was being taken up, all over the country. During the past eight years I have had the pleasure of teaching Sloyd to over three hundred teachers, both men and women. Most of these teachers have been busy in their regular school work, and have often come to the Sloyd lesson at half-past four o'clock in the afternoon, pretty well tired out from their day's task. The Sloyd work, however, in many cases has proved beneficial to them. While I have long believed that a change of work is sometimes a rest, I have been surprised by the number of these teachers who have testified to the gain in muscular strength and in general health obtained from the Sloyd exercises.

Several articles have been published in Swedish on Sloyd in relation to gymnastics. Among others should be mentioned those by Professor Torngren and Professor Key; but nothing so thoroughly good has appeared, I think, as the publication from Nääs, Sweden, entitled " Salomon and Silow Sloyd Positions, with Directions." This work, with charts and illustrations, is the result of careful thought and investigation by Herr Otto Salomon, of Nääs, and Captain Silow, of the Royal Central Gymnastic Institute at Stockholm. As several of the tools shown on these charts differ somewhat from those we are accustomed to use in this country, I hope to be able some time in the near future to make a few changes, and to publish an American edition of the book and charts. I think that these pictures, showing correct working positions and pointing out to teachers the danger of wrong methods of work, ought to be in every Sloyd room, to remind both pupil and teacher of the opportunity and necessity for making manual training a factor in physical education.

VIII.

MANUAL TRAINING.

Paper read at the meeting of the State Teachers' Association at Concord, N.H., Oct. 20, 1900.

It is a pleasure to me to have the opportunity of speaking to teachers on a subject which, because of its educational importance, lies very near to my heart. As assigned to me, the subject is "Manual Training"; but I much prefer to substitute for this expression the one word "Sloyd," which means not only manual, but mental training. I do this because I am unwilling to separate even in words the work of the hand from the work of the brain. I will speak to you, then, if I may, on the subject of Sloyd.

Although I agree in a general way with the humorist who says, "It is better not to know so many things that are not so," nevertheless, because of the accumulated misunderstandings that surround Sloyd, I shall begin by telling you some things that it is not. I wish, at the outset, to guard against certain mistaken notions as to its theory and practice that prevail in many quarters, and interfere with a right understanding of its principles. Sloyd is not a set of objects peculiar to Sweden or to any other country. It is not merely a series of models. It is not a prescribed course of exercises. It is not the use of certain tools. It is not a fixed system arranged for certain grades of schools or for children of certain ages. Sloyd is an educational agent that advances toward a definite aim, and bases its activities upon universal educational principles. Also, Sloyd is tool work so arranged and employed as to stimulate and promote vigorous, intelligent self-activity for a purpose which the worker recognizes as good. It differs from other forms of manual training.

1. In aiming at ethical rather than at technical results, and at general organic development rather than at special skill.

2. In insisting upon the employment of professionally trained teachers instead of persons with merely mechanical skill.

3. In advancing through rationally progressive exercises where the tools are used to produce objects which are not only artistically good, but which are also of special interest through their serviceableness to the worker. Their appeal to the interest must be largely through the good purpose for which they are fashioned. In Sloyd the motive is of supreme importance.

4. In striving after gymnastically correct working positions and in encouraging the use of both the right and left sides of the body.

5. In giving to each individual opportunity to progress according to his peculiar ability.

These points have been emphasized in Sloyd from the days of its beginning in Sweden over twenty-five years ago; and, because they are more or less disregarded in other forms of manual training, I feel that the word "Sloyd" has a peculiar significance, which we cannot afford to ignore. It is needed to indicate something which the term "manual training" does not indicate, and which the words "carpentry," "wood-work," and "shop-work" fail altogether to convey. Many manual training teachers avoid and discourage the use of the word "Sloyd" while they are gradually adopting Sloyd methods and models. Their opposition reminds one of the prejudice once aroused by the term "Kindergarten," which was denounced as a "foreign word," "un-American," etc.; but, fortunately, those who cared for the thing it named held on to it, and now the expressive word "Kindergarten" could not be spared from our vocabulary. It stands for something precious in education, not for something German; and "Sloyd" stands for something precious in education, not for something Swedish.

Since Sloyd is an educational agent, its general aim must be in harmony with the general aim of education, which I take to be the "fitting for life" by the development of power. The education of the schools must supply an element that was not so much needed during the early years of our national existence, for the primitive farm life then furnished a training that is lacking in our present mode of living. We must in some way make good to our children the loss they have sustained, and it is that we may supply this loss that we advocate so earnestly the adoption of Sloyd in our schools. Many of our strongest and wisest men owe their ability and prosperity to the rigorous nurture of their early homes, to the fact that useful manual occupations were their birthright. These occupations were not only of the most vigorous and healthful kind, which called for a high degree of intelligence and forethought, but they were also of a character to strengthen the moral nature through the development of usefulness and helpfulness to others. A community that furnished such an opportunity had, as I have said, less need of manual training in its schools than the people of to-day; for now conditions of living are so changed that bodily activity, of the sort I have mentioned, rarely exists in the home. Cheap, machine-made goods take the place of hand-wrought articles. Handwork, even upon the farm, is reduced to the minimum, while in the city its place is largely usurped by labor-saving inventions. As a natural consequence, our boys and girls suffer. They suffer for the training which quickened the senses, which gave true eyes, steady nerves and hands, as well as strong muscles, and which also developed that sense of responsibility, self-respect, and independence which is the outcome of work recognized by children as useful. We contend that the school should provide this training. The neglect of such provision is a wrong to childhood which can never be atoned for in later life; for "there is a tide in the affairs" of boys and girls (as well as of men) which must be taken at its flood. The period of greatest muscular growth, when the brain is also developing through muscular activity, is that flood-tide; and it is during this period that all children should be provided with carefully considered manual training.

The necessity of utilizing man's physical powers in developing him into a complete being has been recognized for many centuries and by widely separated peoples; and, if it be true, as has been said, that "the duty of each generation is to gather up the inheritance of the past, and thus to serve the present and prepare better things for the future," we cannot neglect the consideration of manual training. More than two thousand years ago the celebrated Chinese philosopher Confucius practised bodily exercises and games, and laid great stress upon self-activity and invention in dealing with his pupils. He enjoined upon them a knowledge of *things* before *words*, and he discountenanced learning by memory only. The cultured Greeks made the bodily training of youth the most important feature of their education. Martin Luther, in his vigorous fashion, contended that every boy should learn some handicraft while at school. The old Swedish catechism contained a sentence which, I regret to say, is omitted in the new. It ran thus: "Work promotes health and wealth, withholds from many a sin, strengthens against many a temptation, and gives consolation and peace of mind in the evil days."

In the teachings of all educational reformers the necessity of bodily training and activity is emphasized. Comenius laid great stress upon it, as did Rousseau, Pestalozzi, Herbart, Fröbel, and Cygnæus.

Neither is the present time lacking in able defenders of the rights of childhood in this matter. Professor William James says, "The most colossal improvement which recent years have seen in secondary education lies in the introduction of the manual training schools,— not because they will give us a people more handy and practical for domestic life and better skilled in trades, but because they will give us citizens with an entirely different intellectual fibre." Dr. G. Stanley Hall, whom you all know, demonstrates the physiological and psychological importance of giving room for the free play of the natural interests of boys and girls in our schemes of education. Professor John H. Tylor, in tracing the evolution of man, shows that education is incomplete without manual training. Indeed, most of the modern physiologists and psychologists demonstrate the value of Sloyd, although they may never use that word.

It was to supply this recognized need that the famous school for the training of Sloyd teachers was established at Nääs.

In harmony with this effort in Sweden the Sloyd Training School which I have the honor to represent was established in Boston. It is a free school for teachers, supported by Mrs. Quincy Shaw. The requirements for admission to the school are graduation from a normal school, or training and experience equivalent to this. The course covers one short school year of eight months, from October 1 to June 1, with five hours, daily session. Nearly two hundred teachers have been graduated from the school during the twelve years of its existence, and most of them are now engaged in teaching the subject in different parts of this country. By an approximate estimate about twenty-two thousand pupils are now (1900) receiving instruction in Sloyd from the graduates of this school.

Externally, American Sloyd may appear to differ from Swedish Sloyd; but in reality they are one, for they are one in principle. Their dissimilarity is only such as must arise from this very principle, which is that *methods* will always vary with varying *conditions*. Nevertheless there is a certain similarity of method (which all who will look below the surface must recognize) characterizing the work of those who hold to the same principle. The Swedish models are objects which Swedish boys take pleasure in making. The models which have been contrived for American boys, some of which I shall show you, are objects which have proved to be of interest to American boys. The test of the value of any course of models is the amount of stimulus which they furnish to the activity of each boy who undertakes to make them.

I trust I have afforded you some arguments that will help establish our claims for the value of Sloyd for all boys and girls in all schools. I am sure that, with the right kind of teacher, the results it will help to produce will be the harmonious and simultaneous development of heart, head, and hand.

IX.

AN ANSWER TO SOME OF THE COMMON OBJECTIONS TO SLOYD.

Read at the meeting of the Marlborough Teachers' Association, Feb. 10, 1902.

I congratulate any community which is planning to introduce manual training into the schools. I believe that every child is by birthright entitled to an opportunity for manual training as a part of his education. I believe, also, that any subject under discussion, whether it be educational, social, political, or industrial, can be satisfactorily settled only when we consider its general effect for the betterment of mankind. The aim of education, briefly and broadly speaking, is to make human beings healthier and happier at the same time that it gives them command of all their powers. This of course is the general aim of education: it should consequently be the aim of manual training. That form of manual training in which I am especially interested, and of which I shall speak to you this evening, is what is called Sloyd.

Sloyd is an educational movement based upon universal educational principles, and having a definite educational aim in view.

It will be seen, therefore, that the first essential for Sloyd is the true teacher; that is, one who is fitted by natural gifts and special training for the care, not only of the human body, but also of human souls. Like other educational movements, it has sometimes failed for lack of this essential. Mechanics and artisans, however skilful and well meaning, are not likely to be the best persons to be intrusted with the education of youth. The true Sloyd teacher must be a student of child life; he must understand children, and know how to appeal constantly to the best that is in them, and how to provide wisely for the vigorous use of growing muscles in such a way as to secure a normal physical development as well as mental alertness, pure taste, and right feeling.

In regard to teachers of manual training Dr. C. Hanford Henderson says: "It is difficult to find men and women of broad culture who can also use their hands. It is very easy to find artisans who are willing to exchange the smaller pay and longer hours of the shop for the pleasanter work of the school-room. They believe very sincerely that the only qualification is the ability to turn out good work. I admire their dexterity, I respect their earnestness; but I say to them, and I say to you, that this is not enough." "His [the artisan's] skill is in handling dead material. What we want is something different from this: it is a man whose thought is on the process, whose cunning is in the handling of the living material, the tissue of childhood."

The worth of a Sloyd teacher is best judged by watching his pupils at work,— by their physical attitude, by their interest, and by the motives which incite them, as well as by their ability in using tools and producing correct work.

What is accomplished should not be commended unless we know *why* it was accomplished and *how*.

Thus, as we have seen, Sloyd is to be interpreted by its aim and principles, and not by its outward expression. Like many of our school subjects, it has both its formative and its utilitarian sides. Perhaps they may be described as follows. On the educational side it may be said:—

1. That Sloyd arouses self-respect, and instills respect for all honest labor.

2. It develops self-reliance, concentration, and the power to make and execute a plan.

3. It develops habits of order, accuracy, and neatness.

4. It develops the æsthetic sense, the power to judge rightly as to beauty of form and proportion.

5. It develops right feeling by stimulating the desire to be useful, and by its appeal to the affections through the cultivation of consideration for others.

6. It strengthens the will by offering such a motive as will induce a boy to work hard, and steadily to overcome increasing but carefully graded difficulties.

In cultivating the senses of touch and of sight it certainly is both educational and utilitarian in its aim; but its more peculiarly utilitarian results are dexterity in the use of tools and the ability and desire to be useful.

In spite of its educational effectiveness, some popular objections to Sloyd are often brought forward. The following are the most common objections to manual training in general, and of course also to Sloyd: —

1. Danger that the ordinary school studies may be neglected by taking time for Sloyd.

2. The large expense involved.

3. Making the education of our children a training which fits them to become artisans.

4. "Why should we have Sloyd, when our ancestors succeeded so well without it?"

Not a single one of these objections, however, is raised by educators who understand the nature of the child and who have a clear knowledge of the educational possibilities of Sloyd.

Since this is true, it is only necessary for me to consider these objections very briefly: —

First. That time can be taken for Sloyd without injury to the common school studies has been proved over and over again in places where the matter has been adequately tested. Even when the time has been taken directly from the ordinary studies, the increased ability to grasp the other subjects has more than made up for the loss of time.

A child who turns from books to tools continues to think. He will think more clearly, and he will reach a more definite end by his thinking, if the problem is before him in concrete form as it is in Sloyd, than if he has to consider an abstract problem such as is given him in books. We should do well to follow Horace Mann's advice, " Give one-half of the school time to creating a desire to learn, and you will teach more than by devoting all to books." In addition to the fact that the pupil's interest is greatest in the concrete problem, it has been scientifically proved that mind as well as body is strengthened by judicious physical exercise. It is also true that, although the overworked student may be earnestly thinking out his Sloyd problem (and I have the testimony of many teachers, themselves students of Sloyd, that this same Sloyd problem in wood costs them more careful thinking than had ever been given to their algebra, Greek, or Latin), nevertheless I believe that the change from hours of sitting still to the vigorous physical activity of Sloyd affords such relief that some of the evils of over-study may be counteracted thereby.

A well-known principal of a high school once said to me that he believed that he could prepare his students for college in half the time usually taken, provided the other half be given to well-directed manual training. Time is thus gained, not lost. Old Bishop Comenius's idea of teaching may be well applied here. " It is to seek and find a method of instruction by which teachers may teach less, but learners learn more, to inspire the children with the love of learning and to bring greater happiness to mankind through active doing."

Second objection: The expense. It is true that the outfit of a Sloyd room costs a good deal, but the running expenses are very light. For a class of twenty pupils the outfit, consisting of the best benches and tools, will cost about $425, and the running expenses about 75 cents a child for the year. In addition to this will be the salary of the Sloyd teachers, which probably will be a little more than that of the ordinary teachers in the community. With such equipment, two hundred children weekly can be taught by one teacher. The time given to each child is generally one lesson a week of two hours.

When the educational value of this subject is understood and appreciated, it will not be difficult to raise funds for it because it will be believed that the money will be well invested. In the country from which I came (Sweden) they not only have Sloyd for the public school-children in the large cities: it is also provided for in the country schools. In Russia, which country we are perhaps accustomed to think of as little interested in educational matters, the so-called Russian method of manual training has been replaced by Sloyd. The Sloyd is prospering in England. Many teachers go to Nääs, Sweden, for short holiday courses; and similar courses are held in various parts of the country under the auspices of the Sloyd Association of Great Britain and England. In Germany there are at present 836 schools and institutes which conduct the manual training on a pedagogical basis. In Canada, through the generosity of one man, Sir William C. Macdonald, of Montreal, provision has been made for Sloyd for three years at one centre in each of the seven provinces, including the expense of qualified teachers. Report has recently come to us that in Chili, South America, a school is established for the training of teachers in Sloyd for the public schools. In the Argentine Republic, also, Sloyd is established. In Porto Rico and various other places it has gained a foothold. From the Commissioner of Education in Cuba has just come the request that we should take yearly at our school in Boston six native Cubans to train as Sloyd teachers for that island. Already four teachers from our school are employed there. If in all these places the expense of Sloyd work has not been too great a burden, surely the people of the United States, whose boast it is that nothing is too good for their public schools, ought to be able to meet the expense.

Third objection: It is a misconception that Sloyd is

chiefly calculated to make artisans and bread-winners: it is a misconception, however, which is sometimes received with great favor. By some persons it is considered a drawback to progress in culture. On the other hand, I have frequent visits from parents of the children at our school who say, "How good it is for my boy to learn all this, so that he can make his own living when he leaves school!" It is difficult to explain to these people just what our object is, because it is natural for certain parents always to look upon the boy as a bread-winner; and, moreover, I gladly admit that he will be better able to make his living when he has had this training than if he had not received it. Nevertheless, the teacher's duty is a far higher one than simply to make of a boy a bread-winner in some specific way. The business of the public school is to train all the faculties of the child, that he may be more ready to grapple with any situation in life; and I firmly believe that a boy who has had good Sloyd training is thereby better fitted not only for an artisan, but also better fitted to become a physician, lawyer, or clergyman because of the improved mental, moral, and physical training he has obtained through his hands. As to Sloyd's being considered a drawback to general culture, I would say this: If a boy learns to use tools, he will not necessarily follow the pursuit of a mechanic; he will not be debarred from rising in the world. Many persons are kept down in this world through ignorance and want of skill; but I have never seen nor heard of any man who was kept down by knowledge and skill rightly employed. To say that to teach a boy the use of tools will force him to become a mechanic is like saying that, if a boy is trained in gymnastics, he must become an athlete, or that, if he is taught to skate, dance, or ride, he must earn his bread by these occupations.

I have already mentioned that it is sometimes urged to its discredit that Sloyd is a new thing which our honorable ancestors did not know anything about, and without which they reached a high state of culture and skill, and had such command of their powers as enabled them to meet any emergency. It is also said that what was good enough for the father is good enough for the son. It must be remembered, however, that the conditions of living are now very different from those of earlier times; that there is hardly any opportunity to engage in those healthy, natural industrial pursuits which were opened to every boy and girl fifty years ago. While we have prospered on the industrial and the economic side through the rapid progress of inventions in the way of machinery, the faculties of the human mind still require the strong and effective nurture characteristic of the olden time, and which the necessities of living then furnished. Our system of education must supply this need if we would produce through it the same strong type of manhood and womanhood.

Perhaps I ought to add that, although I fully believe in the necessity of Sloyd for all our children, I have not said, nor do I believe, that Sloyd is the one remedy for every evil in our schools.

I do believe, however, that it is one of the most effective agents in general education, and that it supplies a need which at present is not filled by anything else.

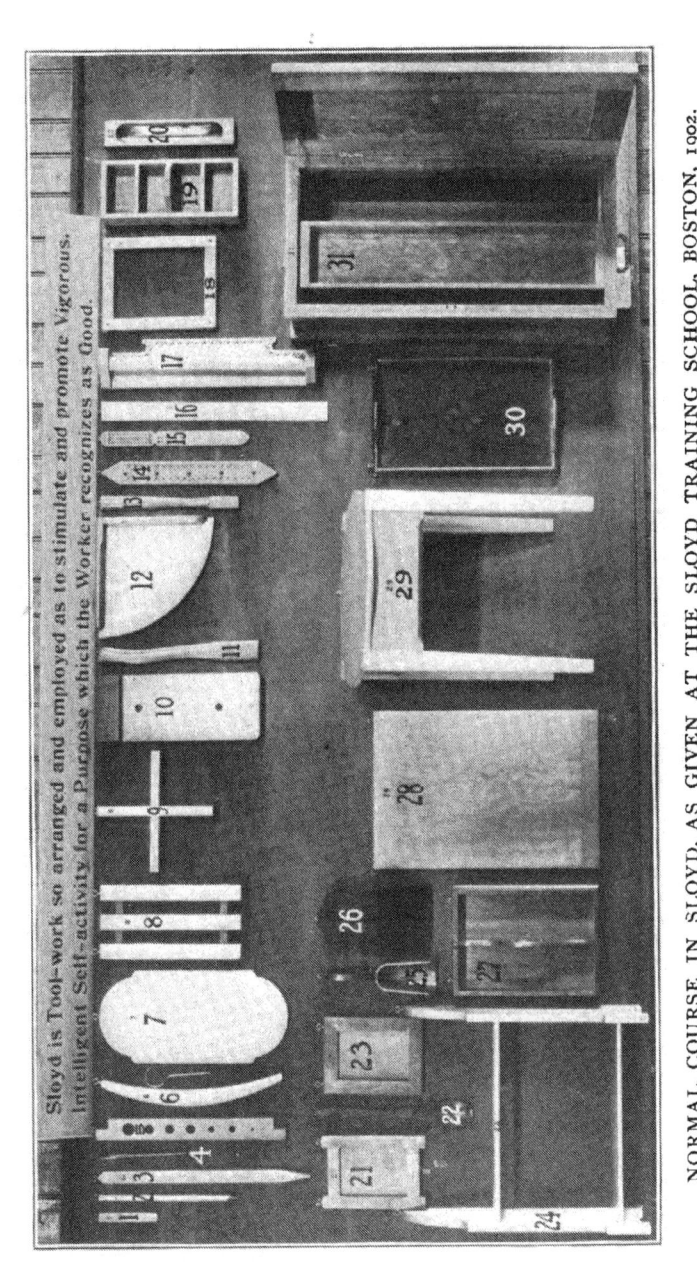

NORMAL COURSE IN SLOYD, AS GIVEN AT THE SLOYD TRAINING SCHOOL, BOSTON, 1902.

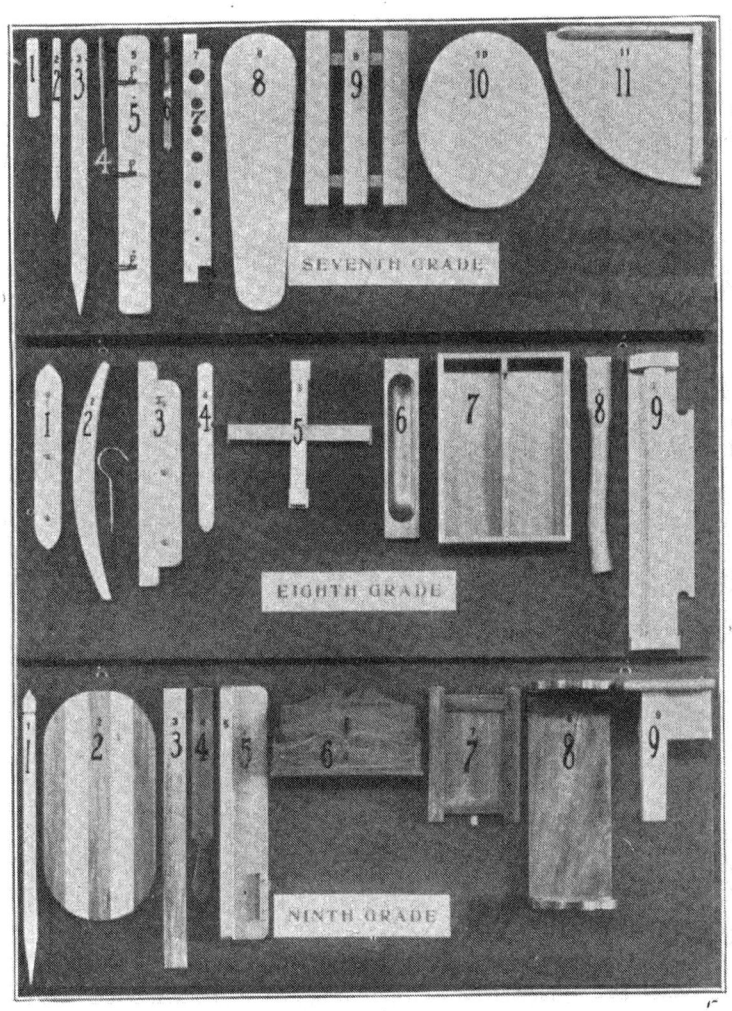

SUGGESTIONS MADE IN 1896 TO TEACHERS OF THE HIGHER GRAMMAR GRADES, WHERE THE TIME GIVEN TO SLOYD IS LIMITED TO TWO HOURS A WEEK.

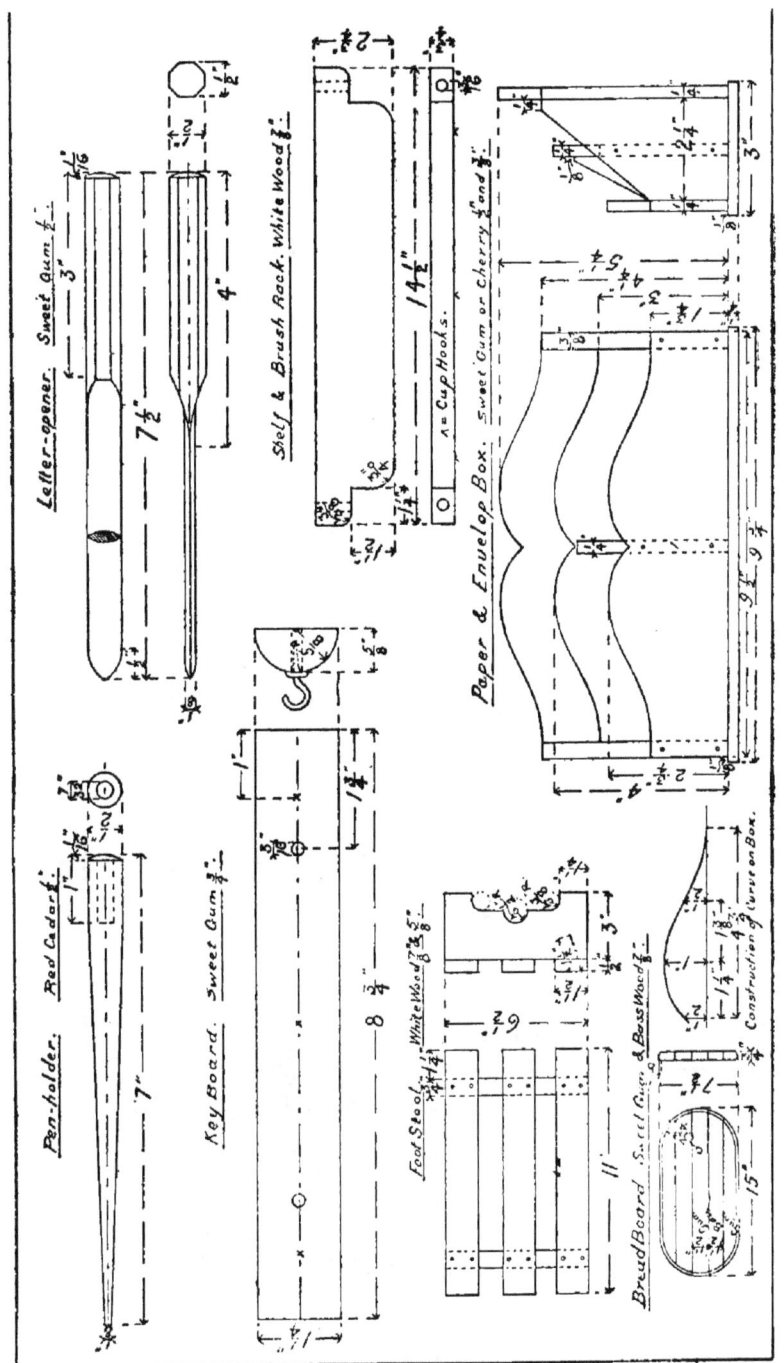

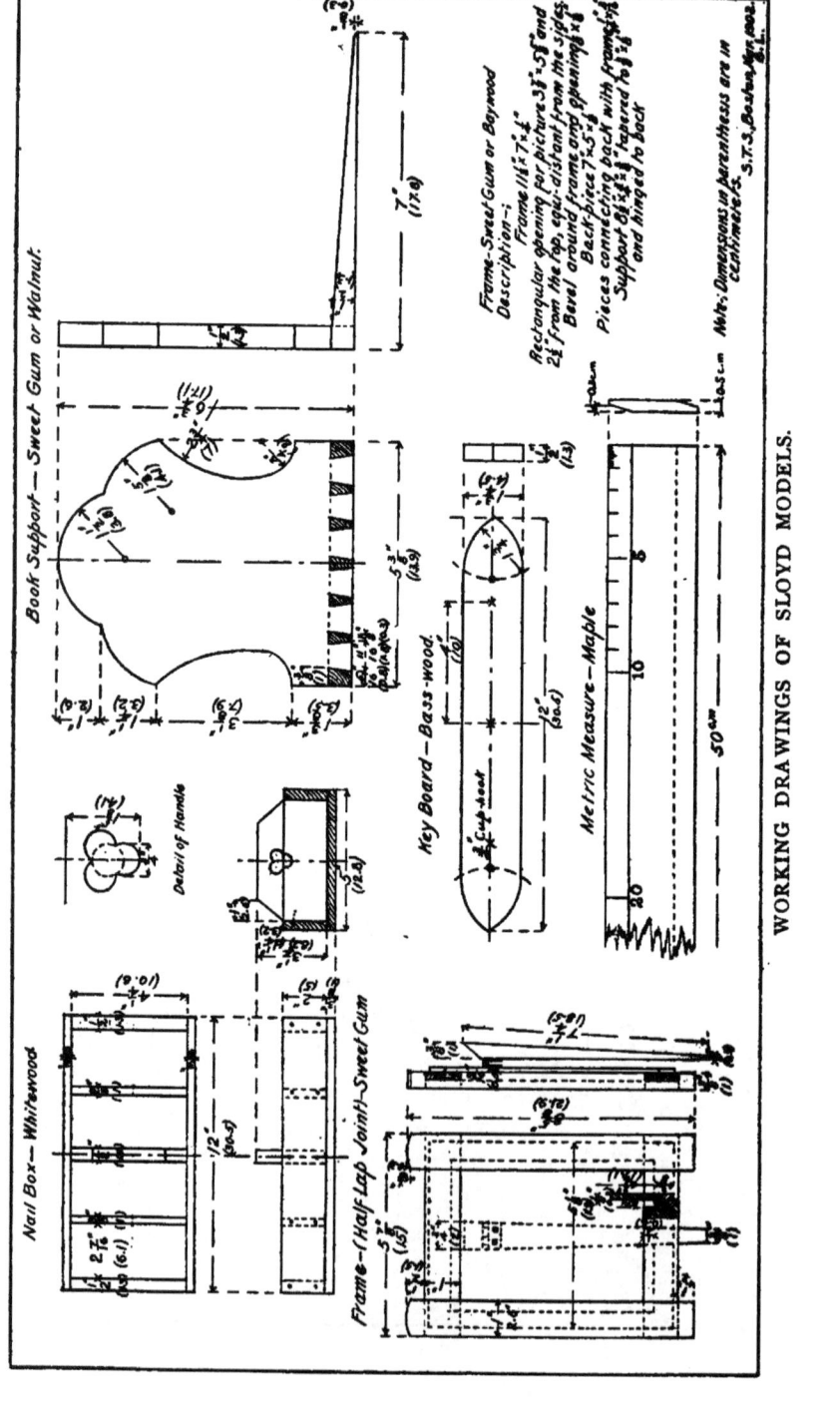

WORKING DRAWINGS OF SLOYD MODELS.

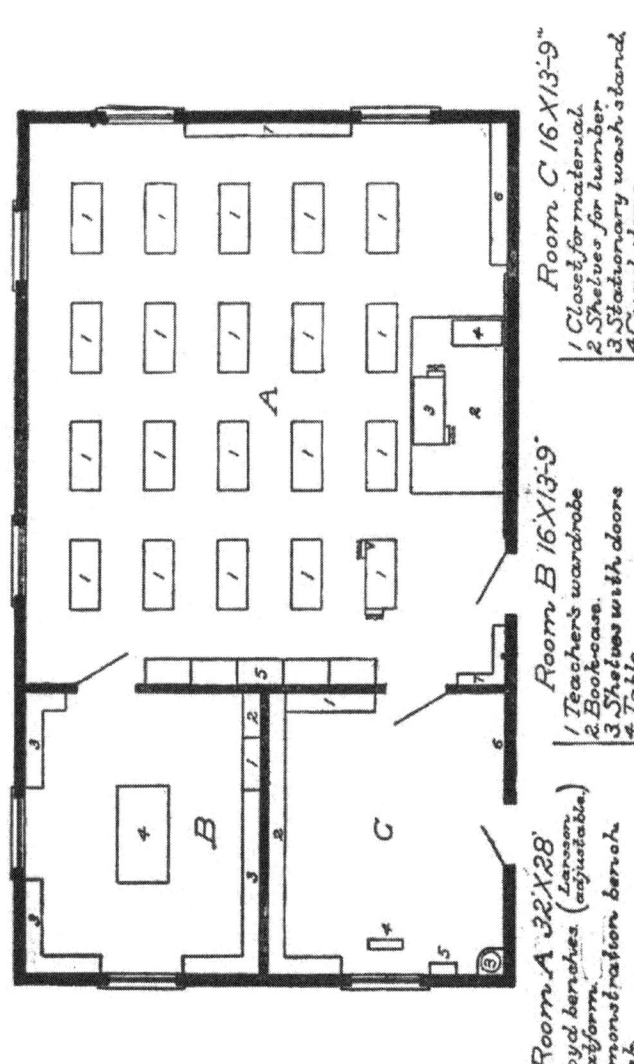

Room A 32'X28'
1. Sloyd benches. (Larsson adjustable.)
2. Platform.
3. Demonstration bench.
4. Desk
5. Pigeon-holes.
6. Closet for material
7. Shelves for general tools
Price of complete outfit (benches & tools)

Room B 16X13'-9"
1. Teacher's wardrobe
2. Book-case.
3. Shelves with doors
4. Table.

Room C 16X13'-9"
1. Closet for material.
2. Shelves for lumber
3. Stationary wash stand.
4. Grind-stone.
5. Shelf for oil-stone.
6. Hooks for clothing.

Sloyd Training School Boston Mass. Gustaf Larsson

CPSIA information can be obtained
at www.ICGtesting.com
Printed in the USA
LVHW052139150520
655578LV00005B/238